The Uddhava Gita

The
Uddhava Gita

Translated by
Swami Ambikananda Saraswati

Introduction by
Thomas Cleary

Foreword by
Prof. Vachaspati Upadhyaya

Seastone

BERKELEY, CALIFORNIA

Published by Seastone, an imprint of Ulysses Press
        P.O. Box 3440
        Berkeley, CA 94703
        www.ulyssespress.com

First published in Great Britain in 2000 by Frances Lincoln Limited

Library of Congress Cataloging-in-Publication Data

Puranas, Bhagavatapurana, Uddhavagita. English
  The Uddhava Gita / translated by Swami Ambikananda Saraswati ;
  introduction by Thomas Cleary ; foreword by Vachaspati Upadhyaya.
    p. cm.
  Includes bibliographical references.
  ISBN 1-56975-320-2 (trade : alk. paper)
  I. Ambikananda Saraswati, Swami. II. Title.

BL1140.4.B4342 U23 2002
294.5'925--dc21   2002026791

Printed in Canada by Transcontinental Printing

10 9 8 7 6 5 4 3 2

COVER IMAGE: *The poet Jayadeva bows before Vishnu*
  (detail from an Indian miniature, Pahari School, 1730)
  Photograph: AKG London/Jean-Louis Nou
  Author Photograph: Steve Dunning
COVER DESIGN: Becky Clarke

❈ Contents

dedicated to my guru
Swami Venkatesananda Saraswati

And the Radiant One, Krishna, said,

I will tell you who is a sage:
One who is compassionate to all beings,
Who harms none,
Who is forbearing,
And whose strength is truthfulness.
One who is free from envy,
Whose mind is poised in both joy and sorrow
And who seeks first and foremost the welfare of all.

(6:29)

❋ Introduction

It is a pleasure to have this opportunity to welcome a genuinely new contribution to the projection of the sacred literature of India in the English language. While countless versions of the *Bhagavad Gita* have been recreated by enthusiasts in recent times, the consummation of this teaching in the *Uddhava Gita* has until now remained virtually unknown outside India.

In terms of religious technology, *Uddhava Gita* represents the method of Bhakti, or devotion, as a path to liberation and Self-realization. While using the temporal expedient of human imagery for divinity, this type of Bhakti is devoted to absorption in the formless universal Self. The essential distinction is therefore made between the empirical self, a subjective notion of the *aham-kara* or " 'I'-maker," and the real Self, an objective reality of an order entirely different from that of any socially constructed identity.

In her admirably restrained commentary on the text, translator Swami Ambikananda Saraswati has made a point of emphasizing this critical distinction between the self and the Self. This is not a mere philosophical nicety, but a most urgent practicality. The ill effects of self-worship in the competitive arena of mundane ambitions grow increasingly evident in the modern day, not only on the individual level, but also on the corporate, national, cultural, and ideological levels of human endeavor.

In the religious field, the adverse consequences of self-worship disguised as Self-worship are also becoming better known to the public, in the socio- and psycho-pathologies of self-deceived gurus and their deluded followers. Greater sophistication in this area would protect civilization more surely from meddlers than mere aversion.

Thus, however ancient, and albeit in unfamiliar garb, in this central respect the present text has a message of much importance for the modern day. While the fallacy of the conventional concept of self is now scientifically well established, the practical implications of this realization have yet to be widely embodied in modern civilizations, which therefore labor under the influence of illusions produced by identification.

While Western ideas of self and identity have generated delusions of grandeur and aggression beyond belief, in one important respect they have had a restrictive effect on individuals and societies. Restricted concepts of human capacities, accompanied by increasing mechanization of life, have dwarfed the scope of perception to the point where organic functions are cramped and distorted by the egotistical attitudes associated with overestimation of the empirical self.

This form of bondage to an unnaturally reduced sense of being has a negative effect on mental and physical health, both individual and collective. The results are manifest in the present day, and it is undoubtedly for this reason that more advanced researches in medical science include study of the dynamics of relationships between psychological and somatic conditions, or subjective and objective states.

In this context, modern civilization could very possibly profit from a sober reexamination of practical implications of supposedly metaphysical concepts such as *maya* and supposedly mystical phenomena such as *siddhi*.

As readers of Indian philosophy are well aware, *maya* means "illusion," and as such is popularly taken to rationalize the identification of liberation with departure from the world. *Maya* also means "art" and "science," however, therein illustrating the constructive potential in the realization that the nature of the world is not objective and elemental but relational and interactive.

Siddhi, often referred to as a mystical or magical power, basically means "accomplishment." The term refers to capacities that are usually left dormant but can be activated by certain specialized usages of the brain and nervous system. True to tradition, the Swami Ambikananda Saraswati has been reserved in her presentation of the chapter on *siddhis* in the present work, as these "extra" capacities are often construed as objects of greed, based on confusion between the empirical self and universal Self. With the proper understanding and experience of *maya*, however, the *siddhis* have tremendous potential for practical application in healing and other modes of human service.

One of the values of the present text is its illustration of the diverse articulations of Bhakti employed to achieve specific results, avoiding the sort of oversimplified devotion that robs its devotees of intelligence. In this respect, the present translation of *Uddhava Gita* is to be welcomed for its contribution to the broadening of information and understanding in an area too often obscured by imagination.

Whereas retellers of the *Bhagavad Gita* have not always bothered to learn Sanskrit or practice Dharma, in this maiden version of *Uddhava Gita* we are fortunate to have an earnest rendering of this text from an individual who has had enough respect for it to have personally made the effort to learn the language and practice the religion.

In this connection, Swami Ambikananda Saraswati has made a point of emphasizing the spiritual interpretation of terms in preference to technical analysis. For those unfamiliar with the nature of Sanskrit and its relation to Dharma, it may be useful to clarify or perhaps expand upon this by noting that the spectrum of Sanskrit semantics has such a range that it can comprehend all fields of human thought and endeavor. Only in sectarian and specialist writings do scientific, cultural, and spiritual ranges of meaning become disparate. This may be useful, even necessary, as a temporary expedient for a specific time and purpose, but it is not in the nature of the language to maintain such distinctions as a permanent feature, to the point that they become obstacles to overall integration of human consciousness, instead of awakening the full range of its positive potential.

As one experienced in Sanskrit translation from Hindu and Buddhist traditions, what I understand from Swami Ambikananda Saraswati's caveats about usage is that she prefers to convey pragmatic semantic sense in context, rather than the sort of alienated, underdeveloped semi-philology to which so many academic grammarians and abstract philosophers have unwittingly fallen prey in their treatment of Sanskrit and other classical linguistic systems.

This seems worth mentioning in view of the possibility that those unfamiliar with the remarkable richness and range of Sanskrit might misconstrue the candor of the translator on this point as mere humility, or misperceive her method as implying technical imprecision, missing thereby the practical purpose of the procedure.

Thomas Cleary, Ph.D.

author of *The Ecstasy of Enlightenment: Teachings of Natural Tantra* and co-author of *Twilight Goddess: Spiritual Feminism and Feminine Spirituality*

❋ Foreword

The Puranas have achieved a place in the sacred and secular literature of India deemed to be next in importance only to the Vedas. Amongst the eighteen surviving Puranas, the *Bhagavatha Purana* is undoubtedly the most outstanding work of devotional literature. It enjoys a popularity next to that of the *Bhagavad Gita*, and has exercised a more powerful influence in India than any other poetical work of its type. So I am glad that this reader-friendly translation of the Uddhava Gita, which forms an important part of the *Bhagavatha Purana*, has been undertaken by Swami Ambikananda Saraswati.

The word Purana connotes "a tradition that exists from ancient times." Sometimes it has been understood as "containing a record of past events." Thus the meaning appears to be "Puranam akhyanam" ~ an ancient narrative. This etymology is important because it signifies the intrinsic value of the Puranas that have been handed down to us. The Sanatana Dharma (the "eternal law," Hinduism) is said to be "shruti smriti Puranokta," meaning "that which is heard, that which is remembered, and the Puranas." The *Chhandogyopanishad* calls the Puranas the "fifth Veda." The *Mahabharata* comments that whoever attempts to study the Vedas without a deep knowledge of the Puranas "frightens" the Vedas. The *Ramayana* mentions the Puranas in a respectful way that shows they were held in high esteem.

According to the traditional view, the Puranas were composed in an easily comprehensible language and style in order to explain to the layman the philosophy and religion of the Vedas and the Upanishads. The Vedas are taken to be "prabhusammit vakya," or "the words of authority," meaning that they are accepted because of shraddha, or faith. The Puranas, however, are "shraddha vakya," or "the counseling of a friend." They teach the message of the Vedas in a friendly way because they are rich in parables and stories.

The Puranas are a veritable mine of information about all aspects of Hinduism. It is encouraging to note that they have generally not sided with any sectarian philosophy or school. They contain the basic principles of the Hindu philosophical schools of Samkhya, Yoga and Vedanta. Aspects of the philosophy later found in Buddhism and

Jainism can also be easily identified, as well as astronomy, astrology, elements of poetics and other valuable material. The Puranas also embody the earliest traditional history. One can even say that Hindu culture and civilization were saved from disintegration and devastation because of their impact. The Puranas gave new aspirations and solace to those who were deprived of many privileges and kept away from spiritual attainment on the flimsy grounds of caste, sex, race and region.

The first Purana to be translated into a European language was the *Bhagavatha Purana*. Eighty-one commentaries on the *Bhagavatha Purana* are available in Sanskrit, and it has been translated into almost all the languages of India. Among the great classics of Indian tradition, it is considered to be the foremost text of bhakti (devotion). It is difficult to specify with any degree of accuracy the date of the *Bhagavatha Purana*, or its authorship. The consensus of opinion is that the Puranas are the creation of innumerable hands, and that their authorship cannot be attributed to any individual. However, the *Bhagavatha* does not show the lack of cohesion or compactness that must mark a work handled by many writers; and the text specifically states that it was written by Veda Vyasa.

It has been well said that the *Bhagavatha* is vangamayavatara ~ the incarnation of the Supreme in the form of literature. Even if we forget, for a moment, its profound philosophy, the *Bhagavatha* can hold its own in the world of literature on the basis of aesthetic quality alone. Here is a poet who uses pattern and metaphor in a complex craftsmanship to create a ritual of celebration.

The *Uddhava Gita* is rightly considered the last message of Shri Krishna. It is a happy augury that a sannyasin has done this splendid job of translating its teaching of the need for renunciation, as Swami Ambikananda has herself renounced worldly pursuits at an early age and was trained under the inspiring guidance of Swami Venkatesanandaji for a proper understanding and realization of vairagya (freedom from worldly desires) and bhakti. She has indeed given yeoman service in translating this text with great devotion.

Swami Ambikananda's success in rendering the work into metrical composition is a tribute to the versatility of Sanskrit and the lucidity of the original writing. The method of her translation is marked by two considerations. She has sought to find close equivalents, keeping in view both the formal and dynamic aspects of the language; and her interpretive translation aims at complete naturalness of expression, pointing the reader to the modes of behavior within the context of his or her own culture.

The introduction and the commentaries on each dialogue will definitely add fresh thoughts to our existing stock of knowledge. Swami Ambikananda has a remarkable acquaintance with the teachings of Bhagavan Krishna, and the knack of putting forth the outcome of her in-depth studies in an impressive manner. Her style is quite easy, unlike that of polemical translation which sacrifices simplicity in the name of precision. This translation is, in my opinion, a valuable contribution to bhakti literature, and deserves to be carefully studied by all serious students of the message given by Bhagavan Krishna. It is bound to open a new spectrum in the understanding of the subtle issues revolving around jnana, bhakti and karma.

I congratulate the translator and the editor of this work on their refreshing achievement, and also the publisher for embarking upon such a pleasant task, which will provide inspiration and solace to many people at a global level.

Prof. Vachaspati Upadhyaya

Vice Chancellor, Lal Bahadur Shastri Sanskrit University, New Delhi

The *Uddhava Gita* comes from a much larger text called the *Bhagavatha Purana*, the "Book of God." Throughout its twelve volumes, the *Bhagavatha Purana* depicts the life and teachings of Krishna, considered to be the eighth incarnation ~ or avatar ~ of the god Vishnu. Of all the incarnations of Vishnu, Krishna alone is seen as a total incarnation.

Krishna is also central to the *Bhagavad Gita*, the famous dialogue between Krishna and Arjuna that is part of the epic poem, the *Mahabharata* (of which the earliest written version dates from *c.* 1400 BCE). Arjuna is a young warrior who suddenly gets cold feet as battle is about to commence and turns to Krishna for advice. In the *Uddhava Gita*, it is Uddhava ~ an old man, and the friend and humble counselor of Krishna ~ who asks for spiritual advice on the eve of the avatar's departure from earth. To fully understand the message of Krishna, we need both the urgent questioning of Arjuna, the young warrior faced with overwhelming odds (as we all are at some point in our lives), and the gentle probing of the wise, older man. It is Uddhava who can negotiate the labyrinth of the spiritual path by asking the pertinent questions. Both texts contain a teaching to which human beings everywhere, who seek a life that more fully reflects the divine, can look.

The origins of Western culture are most often sought in Greece, but they can just as well be sought in India. Sanskrit, the language of the *Bhagavatha Purana*, is the mother of all Indo-European tongues, and many words derived from it are found in all the major languages of Europe. It was India that gave to the mathematicians of Greece the zero ~ which was far from nothing. To the ancient dwellers of the Indus Valley, now popularly known as Hindus, the zero was not only a mathematical symbol but also a representation of the Oneness of creation. India's history is a record of invasions, some friendly and others hostile. One of India's strengths is that all the influences these immigrants brought were continually enfolded into that Oneness. *Om isavasyam-idam sarvam!* ("All is but the one Supreme!") declares the opening mantra of the *Isavasya Upanishad*, the first Upanishad a student of religion in India would learn. On Indian soil, the irreconcilable were reconciled. Dr. S. Chatterji, addressing the 17th All India Oriental Conference in Ahmedabad, said:

> *The fundamental trait of this* [Indian] *civilization may be described as a harmony of contrasts, or a synthesis creating unity out of diversity. Perhaps more than any other system of civilization, it is broad and expansive and all-comprehensive, like life itself, and it has created an attitude of acceptance and understanding which will not confine itself to a single type of experience only, to the exclusion of all others.*[1]

This perspective must be borne uppermost in mind when approaching the *Uddhava Gita* and other scriptures of the Sanatana Dharma (popularly known as Hinduism).

On this soil, ancient systems of worship like Tantra and Yoga flourished, and into these were injected the Vedas, the large body of scriptures that the ancient rishis (seers) considered the paramount religious authority. (The dating of this process is controversial, but some sources give 4000 BCE.) While the Vedas could be interpreted or commented upon, they could never be changed or replaced. They were passed down through an oral tradition known as shruti, which requires the listener to enter a different state of consciousness in which the inner meaning of the truths conveyed in the scriptures is revealed. This allowed the process of revelation to be continued from generation to generation. Only four Vedas survive: the *Rig Veda*, the *Sama Veda*, the *Yajur Veda* and the *Atharva Veda*. The word veda means "knowledge" and the Vedas were said to contain the sum of knowledge required not only for spiritual worship but also for social relations and conduct. They were to form the basis of Hindu religious ritual and dharma, or law.

Time and movement did not stop there. People traveled, cities and civilizations expanded and ideas circulated ~ many of which were enfolded into the Oneness, as the new was eventually embraced by the old. Amidst this sea of change, somewhere between 3,000 and 1,400 BCE, a great movement emerged: the bhakti movement. A new dharma was born ~ the path of adoration and devotion, or bhakti. Initially called the Bhagavatha cult, bhakti is now an integral part of every Hindu's life. Each home will have a shrine for the household "god," the ishta devata (literally, "the chosen deity") before which lights, incense and food are offered.

A new body of scriptural literature arose, called the Puranas, of which the *Uddhava Gita* forms a part. In contrast to the Vedas, the Puranas are said to be smriti ~ that which is remembered. The Puranas depict the life stories of the gods and extol their glories, as well as containing treatises on their ritual worship. Shiva, the third member of the Hindu trinity, has his own Purana; similarly, the Devi, the female form of God, and Vishnu, the second member of the trinity, have theirs. In these Puranas, the ghee (clarified butter), which according to the rituals of the Vedas was offered into the formless sacrificial fire, made way for water, flowers, fruit and perfumes offered to symbols and images of gods.

Did all of this mean that the formless, all-embracing One of the Vedas had been usurped by a colorful and seemingly unending queue of gods and goddesses? Certainly not ~ though it is on this question that most students of these ancient texts begin to become baffled. In sum, different schools of thought developed reflecting essentially three divergent themes: the advaitist (non-dualist) philosophy of Shankaracharya; the vishishtadvaitist (qualified non-dualist) philosophy of Ramanuja; and the dvaitist (dualist) philosophy of Madhava. All of these were reconciled in the bhakti movement: a great body of people who opened their hearts and swept aside all priestly injunctions to stand before their chosen deity and make offerings as their devotion dictated. The supreme motivator of this movement was Krishna Vasudeva.

Krishna proposed that there is no need to set aside the ritual injunctions of the Vedas; rather the devotee should bring adoration and devotion to them and perform the rituals without a desire for gain. That is the meaning of the word bhakti ~ to worship with a love that requires no recompense, and to give the beloved form. The formless One of the Vedas and the multiplicity of gods were thus reconciled in this dramatic movement which is so perfectly expressed in the *Uddhava Gita*.

Krishna tells us, through Uddhava, to be devoted to him. Does he mean the persona of Krishna Vasudeva? Yes and no. Yes, when we are bound to the world of "I" and "you" and "them" and identify with individual personalities. No, when we go beyond that world and experience the One. When we say "I," "mine," "me," we are identifying with a personality that is confined in time and space. When Krishna says "I," "mine," "me," he identifies himself as that which is limitless ~ the One, the Self, the Brahman of the Vedas. Whether Krishna is teaching on a battlefield or in his own palace moments before departing from earth, his message is the same: live life in the spirit of renunciation and devotion. What is it that has to be renounced? Personal gain. What is it that we are to be devoted to? That within ourselves and within each being that is Infinite.

This is an interpretive translation in the tradition of my guru, Swami Venkatesanandaji. It is addressed not to scholars but to spiritual seekers. Sanskrit terms that are not translated are transliterated with a view to pronounceability. The English equivalents that I have chosen are meant to express the spiritual message of the text rather than an analysis of each Sanskrit term. In several instances there are no English equivalents. For example, throughout the text I have translated the word Bhagavan as "the Radiant One." Bhagavan is often used as an epithet for Krishna. Traditionally it is a name applied to those gods who possess power, courage, fame, wealth, knowledge and renunciation. Krishna and Shiva both possess all of these qualities and are therefore addressed as Bhagavan. The word is commonly translated as "Lord," which seems an inappropriate title for India's most prominent avatar, since it is borrowed from Western European medieval feudalism. After trying a few other English equivalents such as "the Divine One" and "the Glorious One," I finally settled on "the Radiant One" because it reflects the concept of the ishta devata and also evokes an image of one who possesses glory ~ divinity which is simultaneously and inextricably both personal and infinite.

Almost universally, translations of ancient religious texts refer to any transcendent spiritual presence as "he." This has two limitations. Firstly, it deprives women of the possibility of ever seeing themselves reflected in the Divine. Secondly, it confines the conception of divinity to the dominant social and cultural contexts. I have not used any references to gender when translating Sanskrit terms for divinity such as Brahman, Jiva and Atman. This is a practice which accords with the original Sanskrit tradition of genderless references to the Self. I have also not translated any of these terms as "God" or "soul," as they tend to conjure up anthropomorphic and Christian images.

The *Uddhava Gita* has many repetitions. Some say this is because it had more than one author ~ but let us leave that discussion to scholarship. The repetitions allow us to learn. If we fail to grasp the lesson in one form, it comes in another. The *Uddhava Gita* is a guidebook on ecology in the most holistic sense of that word, for it applies to all relations among all things, "living" and "non-living." It gives us, as spiritual seekers, a teaching on how to live as human beings in a way that does justice to creation and to That which transcends creation.

Long before he became a world-famous monk, the guru of my guru, Swami Sivananda, was known in India for giving people the scriptures. In those early days, he would often write them out by hand and give them to anyone who was interested. My guru, Swami Venkatesananda, made even more of these scriptures available internationally by translating and compiling them into accessible "daily readings." Their work contributed to the tradition of passing the teaching from generation to generation. It was Swami Sivananda and Swami Venkatesananda who opened my heart to this sacred text, and their teaching that enabled me to undertake this translation, which attempts to convey its message to all spiritual seekers.

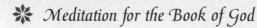 *Meditation for the Book of God*

Srimad Bhagavatham Dhyanam

Om tat sat
Om sri satgurubhyo namah
Om namo bhagavate Vasudevaya

Janmady asya yato 'nvayadi taratas ca 'rthesv abhijnah svarat
    tena brahma hrda ya adikavaye muhyanti yat surayah
tejo varimrdam yatha vinimayo yatra trisargo 'mrsa
    dhamna svena sada nirasta kuhakam satyam param dhimahi

dharmah projjhita kaitavo 'tra paramo nirmatsaranam satam
    vedyam vastavam atra vastu sivadam tapatrayo 'nmulanam
srimad bhagavate mahamuni krte kim va parair isvarah
    sadyo hrdya avarudhyate 'tra krtibhih susrusubhis tat ksanat

We meditate on that transcendent Reality from which this
universe emerges, in which it abides and into which it returns.
On That which is present in all things and transcends all
things, which is self-conscious, full, and which revealed to
Brahma the Vedas which baffle even the best among the sages.
On That through which even the threefold creation, though
unreal, appears to be real by the power of maya which is its own.

In this glorious *Bhagavatham*, given to us by the great sage
Veda Vyasa, is taught the supreme religion free from self-
deception in the guise of desire. In this text has been
expounded the absolute Reality which can be known only by
those free from malice. It is the bestower of supreme bliss and
uproots the threefold agony of body, mind and spirit. Those
who seek that Presence will discover it through this text.

(This is the meditative prayer my guru, Swami Venkatesananda, gave
to his disciples to repeat before studying the text of the *Bhagavatha
Purana*. It helps focus the mind and calm the body.)

The Uddhava Gita

❋ *Dialogue 1*

The first dialogue of the *Uddhava Gita* sets the scene for the teaching of Krishna. The gods, demigods and hosts of angelic beings descend to the city of Dvaraka, where Krishna reigns as prince. Their homage shows the importance of this moment: Krishna, the avatar, the embodiment of Vishnu, is about to leave the world. In this dialogue, Krishna is distinct from both the gods and the assembled people. In succeeding dialogues, he will unfold another view of the avatar ~ as not only an incarnation in a particular time and place, but as a Presence that is in every place, at all times. To come to a realization of that Presence, we have to begin the journey where Uddhava begins it ~ at the feet of the avatar.

An understanding of Krishna's teaching can only begin with an awareness of something greater than our individual selves. The *Bhagavad Gita* begins, on the battlefield of Kurukshetra, with Krishna's challenge to Arjuna's weakness. In the same way, the *Uddhava Gita* opens, in a palace in Dvaraka, when Krishna refuses to take Uddhava away with him. As in the *Bhagavad Gita*, the first dialogue of the *Uddhava Gita* does not contain the teaching itself, but gives its vital context. Like the Yadu clan, we too may squander the teachings, and the opportunities they offer, because we fail to see the precarious position of our own city of Dvaraka ~ a strong fortress built of all our prejudices, pettiness, aggression, limitations, greed. Far better to stand with Uddhava, ready to ask for enlightenment and our own entry into the changeless and eternal realm, Vaikuntha.

The narrator of the story is the sage Shuka, son of the venerable Veda Vyasa, who is said to have first written down the Vedas, the sacred scriptures that had been handed down for centuries by word of mouth. Whether one believes that Veda Vyasa was a person or the name of an office, his role is reproduced here in the character of the sage Shuka. As Krishna's teachings become alive to us ~ wherever we are and whatever our beliefs ~ we too may find ourselves becoming like Shuka, children of Vyasa, ready to pass on this light.

1 Blessed Shuka spoke,

Now Brahma[1] descended to the city of Dvaraka
Where the Radiant One, Krishna,[2] could be found.
Angels of the heavenly spheres and the first born[3]
All went with him.
The great one, Shiva, bestower of blessings,
Also descended down into the city
Surrounded by hosts of spirits.

2 Indra[4] and the wind gods,
Who are the breath of life.
Sons of the goddess Aditi,
Embodiments of social law,
And the attendants of Indra.
The twins of good fortune and health
Who bring healing to the gods.
Those mortals who became immortal
Through the profound skill of their ritual.
The god of magic lore
Who mediates between gods and men,
Along with the god of the first life principle.
Those who govern the means of liberation
And other demigods.

3 The celestial musicians
And the dancing unmanifest potential
Of all of creation.
The ruler of the reptiles.
The perfected ones
And their retinue.
The secret attendants
Of the gods of wealth.
The ancient ones
Who first saw the Vedas.[5]
The ancestors and the
Bearers of wisdom
Who change their form at will,
Along with the celestial half-humans
Who sing to the gods.

⁴ Together these hosts from the heavens
Entered the city of Dvaraka,
Abode of the Prince of the Yadus,⁶
The Radiant One, Krishna,
Who had charmed the world
And whose presence
Washed away all impurities.

⁵ In that dazzling city of Dvaraka,
Replete with the riches of the world,
They gazed upon the Beloved,
The avatar Krishna.

⁶ Covering the prince with garlands
Wrought from heavenly blossoms
They sang his praises.

⁷ The gods sang,

We bow down before you, Beloved Protector.
We bow down before your lotus-feet.
Both those who strive for liberation
And those whose Yoga practice is regular
Hold you in the space of their heart.
As do we.
We prostrate to you with our awareness.
We prostrate to you with our senses.
We prostrate to you with our vitality.
We prostrate to you with our minds.
We prostrate to you with our speech.

⁸ O Flawless One,
By your power of illusion
Spun with the thread of the three phases of nature,
You create, sustain and dissolve this universe.
All this you do within yourself.
Yet you remain untouched and undivided,
Resting eternally in your own bliss.

⁹ O Excellent One,
When the mind is unbalanced
Great austerities and mental disciplines are practiced

Along with scriptural studies and charitable works.
But none of these can confer the balance of mind
That can be obtained
By listening to stories of you
And your life.

10 May your beloved feet
Light the fire that will consume all greed.
May your beloved feet,
Which soften the hearts of sages everywhere
And which they worship for the welfare of all,
Light the fire that will consume all greed.
May your beloved feet,
Which are worshiped by your devotees
And by the wise who seek your company,
Light the fire that will consume all greed.

11 Your beloved feet
Are the very feet contemplated by those
Who make offerings to the sacrificial fire
In accordance with the scriptures;
And by the great Yogis
Who seek to pierce the veil of illusion;
And by the most devout
Who hunger for true knowledge of the Self.

12 O Resplendent One,
The divine goddess of fortune
Rests like a golden streak upon your bosom,
Vying with these faded garlands
That we, your devotees, place there.
Thank you for accepting our worship.
Thank you for the loving kindness
That you extend to all your devotees.
May your beloved feet
Light the fire that will consume all greed.

13 O Infinite One,
Who with a single foot made three strides:
Whose first stride measured the three worlds;
Whose second stride made Ganga flow,

Bathing the three worlds;
Whose third stride ousted the usurper of heaven,
Instilling fear in the unrighteous
And courage in the righteous.[7]
May your beloved feet
Wash away our transgressions.

[14] O Supreme Spirit,
You who are beyond both matter and spirit,
You who are the ruler of time
Before which all embodied beings, even Brahma,
Are led like bulls with a nose ring,
May your beloved feet
Shower us with joy.

[15] O Beloved,
You create, sustain and dissolve this universe,
For you are Purushottama,
The highest with no second.
The scriptures speak of you
As the ruler of nature,
Of spirit and of transformation,
And as time
That becomes the passage of each year.

[16] O Purusha,[8] the Supreme Spirit,
Your power enters the web of illusion
Sowing the seed
From which is born
The golden orb of creation
Enveloped by the seven sheaths:
Earth, water, fire, air, space, ego and mind.

[17] Therefore you are ruler
Of all that moves and all that does not move.
You are ruler of the senses
And supreme authority over the means of action.
Untouched by your creation
You enjoy it as that which dwells within it.
Others, relying on their own limited strength,

Become afraid when they contemplate this world,
Even when they say they have renounced it.

18 You are the one whom sixteen thousand wives
With loving glances and ample charms
Could not disturb.

19 Your glory becomes streams and rivers
Flowing from your feet
Conferring immortality and washing away
The ignorance of the three worlds.
Those who wish to be purified
Can bathe in these waters
By honoring you and your word.

20 Blessed Shuka resumed the story,

After Brahma, Shiva,
And the hosts of gods and demigods
Had thus extolled the virtues of Krishna
They bowed once again.
Then Brahma, ascending to the sky,
Spoke to the Beloved.

21 Brahma the creator said,

O Supreme Soul,
You took human birth
Because we beseeched you
To relieve the burden of the earth.
This you have done to perfection.

22 You have placed the laws of virtuous living
In the hands of the trustworthy and the righteous.
And you have allowed your glory
To be heard by all.

23 By incarnating into this Yadu line,
And assuming a peerless form,
You have taken action
That has illuminated the whole world.

24 In the dark age that is about to descend,
People will have your life and deeds
To light their way to a life beyond ignorance.

25 O Incomparable One,
One hundred and twenty-five years have passed
Since you descended to earth as head of this Yadu clan.

26 O Support of the Universe,
Nothing remains to be accomplished by you.
The wishes of the gods have been fulfilled
And the Yadu line must now submit
To the curse they brought upon themselves.

27 O Ground of All,
If you wish, return now to Vaikuntha,
Your heavenly abode,
And protect us
Who are the servants and guardians
Of that heavenly realm.

28 The Radiant One, Krishna, finally said,

The purpose of my descent has indeed been accomplished.
I have already decided to withdraw from this place
And return to my former existence.

29 This famous Yadu line
Made proud by their many victories,
Is making a bid
To seize all that they see.
But just as the shore stops the ocean wave,
I have stopped their ambition.

30 I cannot leave
Before their destruction is complete
Or they will surely overrun the earth.

31 Through the curse of the brahmins
The destruction of this, my family, has begun.
Brahma, Pure One, before I return to Vaikuntha,
I will sojourn with you for a short while.

32 Blessed Shuka continued,

Being thus addressed by Krishna,
Brahma and Shiva and the hosts of demigods
Prostrated, and withdrew their presence from Dvaraka.

33 The Beloved looked out across the city
And saw the omens of destruction that hung over it.
He turned to the assembly of elders
Of the Yadu clan and addressed them.

34 The Radiant One, Krishna, said,

Look well upon these disturbances all around us ~
Nothing can now halt the curse of the brahmins.

35 Respected elders, nothing will remain here.
In order to survive
You must retreat with me now
To the sacred place, Prabhasa.

36 Through the waters of this place
Even Chanda, the moon, cursed by Daksha,
Was restored and resumed her passage
Through the night sky.

37 We too will bathe in its sacred waters
And make offerings of water and tasty foods
To the ancestors and the gods.

38 We will feed those that should be fed
And through our sacrifice and charity
We will prevent this great calamity
From descending on our heads also.

39 Blessed Shuka resumed the story,

The Yadu elders, advised by their prince,
Immediately began to yoke horses to chariots,
Making ready for their departure from Dvaraka.

40 Watching the Yadu elders,
Seeing the dark portents
And listening to Krishna's words was
Uddhava, the ever-devoted.

⁴¹ Uddhava, the servant, approached the Supreme One.
He prostrated, placing his head upon those blessed feet.
Then he joined his hands over his heart and spoke.

⁴² The devotee Uddhava said,

Ruler of the gods,
Master of all Yoga,
You whose renown is sung everywhere,
I see that you are about to leave this world
And thus seal the fate of the Yadus.

⁴³ Beloved slayer of the demonic,
I cannot bear to be separated from you
And the worship of your holy feet.
Beloved, I beg you, take me with you
Wherever you are going.

⁴⁴ O Krishna, the life you have lived
Has uplifted humankind.
Hearing of it, people renounce greed.

⁴⁵ Dear One, how can your devotee,
Who thinks only of you
Whether lying down, sitting, walking,
Coming or going, bathing or eating,
Live without you?

⁴⁶ We, your servants, inhale the fragrance
Of the garlands you have worn.
We touch your clothes
And handle your adornments.
We even eat the remnants of your food.
We do this to overcome our ignorance.

⁴⁷ Naked sages, lifelong celibates,
Who have pacified their senses
And renounced this world,
Attain the elusive goal of spiritual liberation.

⁴⁸ But what of us who are in this world
And involved in all its works?
We talk of you among ourselves,

We know that you are the guiding light
That will lead us out of darkness.

49 Remembering you,
Recounting your deeds and words,
We, your devotees,
Watch eagerly all your movements,
Your smiles and your glances,
That bring you so near to us
Who are but human.

50 Blessed Shuka said,

The Radiant One, Krishna, the Beloved,
Listened attentively to his devotee, Uddhava.
And then he spoke to him.

❋ Dialogue 2

The teaching commences in earnest when, refusing Uddhava's request, Krishna begins to tell him how to live in the world. The essence of Krishna's message of renunciation is summed up in Verse 6, and its astonishing nature is revealed further in the succeeding verses. Renunciation consists of serving others and, at the same time, letting go of our attachments to them, by being constantly aware that the world is not as we experience it. Behind the veil of multiplicities that present themselves to us as family, friends, other people and nature, there is just One: an all-embracing Self of which everything is part. This idea brings us face to face with the concept of infinity. Was there a point when this universe came into being, and will there be one when it ceases to be? Krishna keeps reminding Uddhava that these beginnings and endings are illusory, just as he reminds Arjuna in the *Bhagavad Gita*: "The Self is not born, nor does the Self ever die." (2:20).

To illustrate this teaching, Krishna introduces the story of the avadhuta. The word means "a pure one" ~ someone who is cleansed of misconceptions and has experienced the reality behind life's veil of multiplicities. The avadhuta is also a sannyasin, one who has decided to live in the spirit of renunciation that Krishna describes. We must be cautious here to ensure that our interpretations do not interfere with the teachings. Krishna advocates not a life deprived of human contact or self-righteous withdrawal but that we ourselves become "a pure one." The story of the avadhuta demonstrates that in all our relationships we should not be attached to the idea we have of ourselves or others but rather constantly seek the eternal in both. A life like this is not devoid of love but filled with it ~ because love is then no longer confined to our own satisfaction.

The king addresses the young avadhuta by the respectful title, brahmin. It would be well to note here four words that sound similar and have the same Sanskrit root but which are very different ~ brahmin, brahmana, Brahma and Brahman. A brahmin or brahmana is a person who belongs to the caste of priests and teachers. Brahma is one of the trinity of Gods composed of Brahma the creator, Vishnu the preserver and Shiva the transformer. Brahman is the term used to describe that omnipresent, all-embracing Presence, the Self.

1 The Radiant One, Krishna, said,

You are right, O fortunate friend,
I am returning to my heavenly realm,
Just as Brahma and Shiva asked me to.

2 I have fulfilled the wish of the gods:
Righteousness has been restored.
It was for this that I became embodied
With that other radiant Self,
Which took the form of Balarama.[1]

3 I have watched as this Yadu dynasty
Came under a curse
Brought on by their own aggression.[2]
They will completely destroy themselves
And this city will disappear with them.
In just seven days
It will be submerged by a deluge.

4 Noble friend,
When I leave this world
Darkness will descend:
The dreaded Age of Kali[3] will begin ~
The age in which all that is auspicious
Becomes hidden and obscured.

5 Do not remain here when I have gone.
You are a worthy soul,
But in this darkness which is to come
People will indulge in all that is unworthy.

6 Shake off all attachments
Whether to family or friends.
Roam the world as one free of all attachments,
With impartial vision.
To do this
Fix your mind on me.

7 Whatever you see, hear or touch ~
Know that you cannot know it
For what it is.

Know that whatever your mind makes of it
Is like a mirage that will fade away.

8 A confused mind sees a world of multiplicities,
A world of good and bad.
This creates a compulsion to act
Or to refrain from acting,
Depending on what will bring gain
And what will cause loss.

9 Therefore, control your senses and your mind.
See this entire universe as the Self
And see this Self in me,
Its supreme sovereign.

10 In this way you will come to know
And realize that the Self within you
Is the same Self of all embodied beings.
Once you know this
Your mind will be completely satisfied
And all obstacles will be removed.

11 One who has thus transcended good and bad
Will act for the good and refrain from acting for the bad,
But not because of any notion of loss or gain.
Rather, these wise ones
Are like children and act without guile,
Doing what has to be done.

12 Such a one is a friend to all,
Filled with peace
Through knowledge of the Self.
Such a one sees this universe
As none other than the Self resting in me.
Such a one is free
From this cycle of birth and death.

13 Blessed Shuka said,

Having heard this instruction of his beloved,
And desiring to learn more,
Uddhava fell again at Krishna's feet and spoke.

14 The devotee Uddhava said,

Master of Yoga,
The very embodiment of Yoga
And the ultimate outcome of Yoga.
You who bestows the power of Yoga
On even the unqualified,
For my salvation,
You have taught the path of renunciation,
The high road of sannyasa.

15 Beloved and All-embracing One,
I think this path of renunciation is a difficult one,
Even more so for those who are committed to this world
And have not yet become devoted to you.

16 I am but an ignorant man,
Firmly attached to this body,
Which I perceive as "my" body
Through the power of illusion,
Which you have woven into your creation.
I am completely immersed in the ideas-of-"I" and -"mine."
Given this, renunciation will be most difficult for me.
I am your servant:
Teach me, Beloved,
In order that I may carry out these instructions.

17 Even among the gods
There is no teacher equal to you,
Who reveals the ultimate truth to your devotees.
Such a teacher is difficult to find.
For even Brahma and all the gods
Are committed to the illusion you have created:
That the perceived world is a reality.

18 Therefore, with my mind burdened by sorrows
And tired of this world, I turn to you,
The Perfect One,
Infinite, eternal and omniscient,
The deity who dwells in changeless Vaikuntha,
The much loved Narayana,4 friend of all.

[19] The Radiant One, Krishna, said,

In this world, dear friend, there are those
Who by their own efforts
Have realized the truth
And ceased craving for material things.

[20] The Self is the real teacher of all people,
Who are endowed with an intelligence
That is able to discern the real from the unreal.

[21] The Self is most easily realized
In the human form.
Through Samkhya and Yoga[5] ~
The path of knowledge
And the path of action ~
I can be experienced as the Self of all,
The power of all,
Manifest in all.

[22] In this world there are many different kinds of bodies:
There are one-legged and two-, three- and four-legged,
There are even those with more than four legs
And yet others with no legs at all.
Of all these forms it is the human form
In which the Self can most easily be attained.

[23] It is here, in this human body,
That I may be discovered as the Self ~
But not by the ordinary means of perception
That are used to understand the world,
Such as assumptions based on evidence and
Inference drawn from certain indications.

[24] To make this teaching more clear
The ancients tell the tale
Of a dialogue between a Self-realized avadhuta
And one of the bygone kings of the Yadu people.
Let me tell it to you now.

[25] This Yadu king chanced upon an avadhuta
Who, though young in body,
Appeared to be endowed with great wisdom.

The king himself was a learned man
And so he approached the avadhuta
With the intention of learning from him.

²⁶ The Yadu king said,

"O brahmin, I see you are not engaged in any religious activity
And yet you seem possessed of extraordinary wisdom.
Enlightened as you are, roaming this world as free as a child,
Where and how did you obtain this clear-sightedness?

²⁷ "Generally people work
Towards some kind of religious merit,
Or towards wealth and pleasures.
It seems that even those
That live a life of seeming self-enquiry
Do so only for the fame and fortune it will bring them,
Or even for the years it will add to their life.

²⁸ "You are a handsome young man
Clearly learned and able-bodied,
You speak well and seem to be quite skilled,
And yet you do nothing.
Nor do you seem to covet anything.
In fact, you behave as if you were a fool or a lunatic or,
Some might say, as if you were possessed.

²⁹ "It seems that while others are being burned
By the wild fire of greed and lust
You remain unscorched ~
Like the elephant that takes refuge in the Ganges
While a forest fire rages.

³⁰ "Pray, tell us, O brahmin,
Who roams this world alone
Without kith or kin to comfort you,
What is the source of your ecstasy?"

³¹ The Radiant One, Krishna, continued,

The young brahmin,
Honored by the Yadu king's respectful attitude,
Deigned to reply.

[32] The brahmin said,

"I have many teachers, O king.
Through my own awareness I have learned from them all,
And now I wander about this earth free from its turmoil.
Let me tell you of my teachers.

[33] "The earth, air and space,
Water and fire,
The sun and moon,
The dove and the python,
The sea,
The moth and the bee,
And the elephant.

[34] "The honey gatherer,
The deer and the fish.
The prostitute Pingala
And the osprey,
The infant and the maiden.
The man who makes arrows
And a certain serpent,
The spider, and the insect
Captured by the wasp.

[35] "These, great king, have been my teachers,
They number twenty-four in all.
From them and their ways
I have learned all that I know,
And all of it has been to my benefit.

[36] "Hear me well, son of Yayati, grandson of Nahusha,
As I tell you what I have learned from these my teachers.

[37] "From the earth I learned to remain undisturbed
Even while being oppressed
By those under the sway of their own destiny.
The earth taught me not to deviate
From the course that I set for myself ~
Just as it does not deviate
From its path around the sun.

38 "As a disciple of this earth
I learned from its lofty mountains
That my movements should be guided
By the service and care of others.
As a disciple of this earth
I learned from its upright trees
That my life should be spent
In sweet dedication to the welfare of others.

39 "From the air I learned
What it means to be an ascetic:
To take only what is needed
To keep body healthy and mind balanced,
And that more than that
Causes mind and body to waste away.

40 "From the air I learned
What it means to be a Yogi:
To move about freely in contact with all things
But attached to no thing;
To be the breath that comes and goes
Unconcerned with reward or punishment.

41 "From the air that moves I learned
That the Yogi comes and goes through many bodies,
Yet remains in untouched stillness ~
Just like the gentle breeze
That carries fragrances from place to place.

42 "From the vast space spread out as the air all around us
I learned of my true identity.
I learned that though clothed in a body
Of one form or another,
All things, moving and unmoving,
Are without boundaries:
For the unlimited Self is present everywhere in everything,
Just as air is present everywhere and in everything.

43 "From space I learned
That the Self remains untouched
By the form that it takes on,

Whatever that form might be ~
Fire, earth or wind ~
Just as space remains untouched
By the clouds blown by the winds.

44 "From water I learned
That the sage must be transparent.
And like water we must be sweet,
Always offering purity
So that others through our company
May be cleansed and purified.

45 "From fire I learned how to burn brightly
Through the power of practice.
From fire I learned we need only the food
That the belly can burn now.
From fire I learned
To accept what is given to me,
And to let the fire of my practice
Transform what is impure and make it pure.

46 "From fire I learned that
In order to teach
The sage must sometimes be hidden
And sometimes be visible.
In this way, like fire,
The sage can grant blessings,
In which all transgressions are burned.

47 "I learned that just like fire
That has no shape of its own,
But to reveal itself
Takes the shape of the log being burned,
So are we.
Whatever our form,
Whatever our history,
The Self reveals itself in all forms
Over and over again.

48 "Time and its passage belong to the body ~
Not to the Self of all bodies.

I learned this by watching the moon,
Which remains the same
Even while it appears to change
With the passage of time.

49 "Through the power of time
Death follows birth
And birth follows death.
Yet the Self does not observe these changes ~
Just as the observer
Does not see each flame of the fire
Being born, taking shape
And dying, to be born again.

50 "From the sun I learned non-attachment.
The sun draws water up into the atmosphere
And then returns it as the gentle rain.
This is surely what it means to live as a Yogi ~
Accepting the experiences that are freely offered,
And letting them go when they are withdrawn.

51 "Like the sun the Self is one.
But like the sun reflected on moving water
The Self appears to be broken into many forms.
But I learned from the sun
Not to mistake the image for the reality.

52 "From the gentle dove I learned
Of the pain that follows obsessive attachment ~
The great torment it brings
And how that torment unbalances the mind.

53 "A dove built a nest
In a tree in the forest
And there he lived with his beloved
For many years.

54 "Their loving hearts became bound one to another
Just as their bodies were bound together in love.
They lived in perfect harmony,
Always seeing eye to eye.

55 "Each intent on the other
They ate, talked, played and slept together
There in their home deep in the forest.

56 "Whatever his mate desired, O king,
This dove would strive to bring her,
No matter how difficult,
For in all things she pleased him greatly.

57 "As time passed the female dove
Laid her first eggs in their nest ~
While her partner watched over her.

58 "At the proper time
And fashioned by that inconceivable Self,
Fledglings with delicate limbs covered by soft down
Emerged from their shells.

59 "The parents took great delight in their offspring.
They loved the gentle cooing and chirping of their children
And showed them every affection a parent can.

60 "They rejoiced to watch their children at play,
To see their first cautious attempts at flight.
And they loved their soft, sweet wings
And their gentle song.

61 "These two, completely content
With their nest and their new family,
And charmed by this illusion
Gave no thought to anything else
Beyond the world they already knew.

62 "One day, as good parents
They left the nest for the entire day,
Seeking out the best food
To bring home to their family.

63 "But on that day a fowler entered the forest
And happened on the doves' nest.
Seeing the young birds at play,
He threw his net and seized them all.

64 "The parents returned by and by
Eager to give their young the tidbits
They had sought out just for them.

65 "The mother dove,
Seeing her young captured and in distress,
Flew to them weeping.

66 "Rushing to her children,
Distracted by grief
And tied to them by love born of illusion,
She herself became entangled in the net.

67 "The father dove,
Seeing both his children
And his beloved partner
Caught in that cruel net,
Broke down in tears.

68 " 'Oh no,' he wailed,
'Behold my ruin ~
I was a fool to let this happen,
This destruction of my family
That was the source of my virtue, wealth and fulfillment.

69 " 'My beloved wife,
To whom I was everything,
Is now going to heaven with our sweet children ~
Leaving me here alone.

70 " 'My life has lost its purpose.
I no longer wish to live in this empty nest
Alone and miserable.
What is there left to live for?'

71 "Unable to bear seeing his family
Dying ensnared in that net,
The dove flew down to them
And was himself captured.

72 "The ruthless fowler,
Having trapped the dove

Who was a devoted husband and father,
Along with the mother and her children,
Tied them up and went home.

73 "Like the dove of my story,
Anyone who becomes so attached
To those things that feed the senses,
Who fails to see that which is
Beyond both joy and sorrow,
Will come to the same end.

74 "We have to soar high
To attain this precious human birth,
Which is like an open door to liberation.
We must not act like the dove,
And fail to look towards that
Which is beyond our home and family."

�֍ *Dialogue 3*

In this dialogue, Krishna continues to relate what the young avadhuta learned from his twenty-four teachers. He concludes with the tale of Pingala, an entirely different sort of teacher from the doves who failed to look beyond the present moment. Pingala is a prostitute who becomes disenchanted with her life and begins to see beyond it to the Self within, which, unlike the body, is not constrained by time.

Pingala's disenchantment is the writing on the wall for all of us. It seems that at birth we forget who we are. Then, as if to make up for this loss of Self-awareness, we seek to gain from the world we perceive through our senses. The poignant description of Pingala preparing herself by day in order to sell herself by night is a description of our lives. In the brightness of youth, we engage in all manner of work, making a place for ourselves in the world. Then, as we enter middle-age and begin the walk towards not the future but a dark and certain death, that place begins to look lackluster. It is then that we undergo what the great sage Patanjali called pratyahara, withdrawal. This does not mean running away from the world (as Krishna repeatedly warns, this is not even possible). Withdrawal simply means looking in a different direction ~ turning our gaze away from ephemeral things towards the unchanging horizon of eternity.

Through the stories of his teachers, the young avadhuta describes the path of renunciation. He gives a code of conduct for those who wish to live as sannyasins, and describes their responsibilities to the community. The role of sannyasin is a sacred one, which in India is held in high honor ~ so much so that the community takes on the responsibility of feeding the sannyasin. The avadhuta points out the seriousness of this mutual undertaking. The central message of renunciation is that no matter where we are or what we do, living a spiritual life means letting go of who we think we are (and of what we think others are) and seeking out the truth. Then, like Pingala, we can go within, where ~ regardless of the events in our lives, good or bad ~ nothing interrupts the search for truth and the peace that search imparts.

¹ The young brahmin continued,

"O king, the pleasure and pain
That we experience through the senses
Come unsought in this life.
Through them we will experience
Both heaven and hell on earth.
The wise know this
And refrain from searching out either.

² "The wise one should be like a python
That does not search out food
But takes only what comes its way ~
Whether it is sweet or bitter.

³ "Like the python when no food presents itself,
The wise one should endure many days
Without sustenance and without striving,
Accepting that this is simply destiny.

⁴ "In this way the wise
Maintain a peaceful body
And an awakened mind,
Not using their strength and vitality
To chase after things that will pass away.

⁵ "Like the full and calm ocean,
The sage should always be tranquil and deep,
Difficult to fathom and to cross,
With an inner awareness
Of the immeasurable
And imperturbable Self.

⁶ "Like the full and constant ocean,
Which remains always the same
Whether the rivers of the earth
Flow into it or not,
The sage should remain in that awareness,
Even as joys and sorrows come and go.

⁷ "Those who fail to control the senses
Are not sages.
They become agitated and disturbed

Even by illusory sexual attractions,
Towards which they plunge blindly,
Like the moth into a flame.

8 "Those who are foolish people
Are easily tempted
By sex, gold and luxurious clothing,
Seeing in them the ultimate pleasure,
They will be burned
Just as the moth is burned by the flame.

9 "Like the bee gathering honey
From many blossoms,
Those who aspire to be sages
Must take just a little to sustain themselves
From all the many sources that life offers.

10 "Like the bee gathering honey
From many blossoms,
Those who aspire to be sages
Must take something of wisdom
From all the scriptures ~
Both the great and the small.

11 "But unlike the bee that hoards
The honey it has gathered,
The sage must never store
More than the hands
And the stomach can hold.

12 "The sage must not store
Even for the evening or the next day.
For like the bee
Both sage and store will be plundered
As the honeybee's hoard is plundered
By those collecting honey.

13 "A sannyasin must refrain
From sexual relationships,
Indeed, even from those things
That would inflame such passions:
Or else they will bind you

Just as easily as the mighty elephant
Can be bound by the trainer's rope.

[14] "A sannyasin should avoid sex
As others avoid death:
For it will kill the path of practice,
Just as an elephant is killed
By the hunter with powerful weapons.

[15] "Wealth accumulated through pain and struggle
And hoarded in safe-keeping
Can bring only pain.
Indeed wealth hoarded
Waits to fill the thief's pockets,
Just like honey
Waiting to fill the honey thief.

[16] "Like the honey gatherer,
The sannyasin receives
Only the first serving
Of the householder's hard-earned produce.

[17] "The sannyasin, roaming the forests,
Should not be drawn to sensual music,
Remembering always the lesson of the deer
Who was lured by the hunter's tune.

[18] "There was a sage's son
Who took the form of a deer,
And was captured by a woman
Whose music wafted to his forest hermitage.

[19] "In the same manner,
A fool seeking to satisfy
A greedy tongue
Will taste death
Like a fish
Biting on a hook.

[20] "For the sage
The sense of taste
Is more difficult

To control
Than all the other senses.

21 "If all the other senses are controlled
But the sense of taste is not controlled,
Then the sage has not yet mastered the senses.

22 "Now hear, great king, what I learned
From the prostitute Pingala,
Who lived in the city of Videha.

23 "As was her habit, Pingala spent all day
Decorating herself for the night.
When night fell,
She went outside
To sell herself to passersby.

24 "As men came and went,
Pingala, greedy for wealth,
Invited them in,
Imagining they had money to spend.

25 "But the men continued on by,
And still Pingala waited,
Sure that a rich man would come along
And make all her work worthwhile.

26 "Deep into the night
She waited without sleeping,
Tired and frustrated
Walking about listlessly.

27 "Thirsty and hungry,
Pingala finally despaired
Of making any money that night.
But her desolation was not in vain ~
For Pingala began to reflect on her life.

28 "Through that lonely vigil
Pingala felt the sharp pain of disgust
For the life she was leading.
Such pain often becomes the sword
That cuts through material longings

And awakens dispassion.
Hear from me the song
That the prostitute Pingala sang to herself.

[29] "For no one, O great king, in whom a disgust
For things of this world
Has not arisen,
Seeks liberation.
It is from this disgust that discernment arises
And the ideas-of-'I' and -'mine' are challenged.

[30] "Pingala sang,

'Alas, I suffer the pains
Of an uncontrolled mind.
What a fool I have been
To believe that happiness
Can be gained
From the men that I solicit.

[31] " 'I have been a fool
To neglect the immortal Self
That resides within my own heart.
It is that Self which is most precious to me,
Which bestows true and eternal wealth ~
Not these poor wretches
Who can give me only their grief and sorrow,
Their fears and worries
Mingled with their infatuation.

[32] " 'Through prostitution
I have tortured this Self.
I expected riches and pleasure
By selling my body
To these pitiful wretches,
But I have gained nothing.

[33] " 'This body is but the house
In which the Self dwells for a time.
It consists of bones and limbs
Covered with skin, hair and nails.
It emits foul odors

And has nine exits for waste.
Who would value it but me?

34 " 'In this city of Videha,
I am the most foolish of all,
For I expected bliss
From something other than the Self.

35 " 'To that dear friend,
That beloved Self that is supreme,
Situated within the heart of all embodied beings,
To that Self, I, Pingala the prostitute,
Will now surrender.
And like the great goddess Lakshmi,
I shall be blissful
Only in the company of the Supreme.

36 " 'For truly, what real joy
Can women rely on
From things
And men
And gods?
In the end all of them
Are devoured by time.

37 " 'Despite the life that I have led,
The supreme One has smiled on me.
From my despair
For what this world has to offer,
Detachment has arisen in my heart.

38 " 'Had I been truly unfortunate
This despair of the world
Would not have been born in me.
This unhappiness enables me
To renounce my expectations
And gain peace.

39 " 'With complete love and devotion
I accept this gift
That has been bestowed on me.
I renounce the pursuit

Of all worldly things,
Taking refuge in the supreme Self.

40 " 'Placing all my faith in this Self,
I shall live a life of contentment
Whatever comes my way ~
With only that Self for my companion.

41 " 'When we are fallen
Into the mire of worldliness,
Blinded by our own senses
And being devoured by the serpent time,
What but the Supreme can save us?

42 " 'When we observe time
Eating away at all things
We begin to see the world
For what it is
And we renounce it,
Realizing that the Self is our only protector.' "

43 The brahmin said,

"Having made up her mind
About the life she wanted to live,
Pingala let go of her hopes and expectations
And retired indoors.

44 "Expectations of this world
And the people in it,
Are surely the sources
Of our greatest misery.
Pingala let these go,
And retired in peace."

✤ *Dialogue 4*

In this dialogue, Krishna finishes his account of the teaching of the young avadhuta. He discusses the necessity of solitude, the importance of practice and the aim of human birth.

The Sanskrit words maya and guna appear here for the first time. There are no real English equivalents for these words. Maya comes from the Sanskrit root *ma*, meaning "to measure," "mete out" or "mark off." Maya can be said to be that by which we measure, limit and confine ourselves and all of creation. The minute I say "I," referring just to the body and personality that appear in a certain time and space, I am functioning under maya. It is most commonly translated as "illusion," as in the preceding dialogues. Maya is the illusion inherent in the world, by which we constantly seek to limit the limitless.

Guna is usually translated as "mode of nature." The word guna actually means "a thread" or "a rope"; and it is the gunas that hold us in bondage to maya. There are three gunas ~ rajas, tamas and sattva. Tamas and rajas correspond to the Yin and Yang of Chinese philosophy. Rajas is the bright, expanding, outgoing force of nature, while tamas is the dark, contracting, ingoing force. When these two are brought into equilibrium, a state of sattva is said to prevail. Only when a state of sattva has been reached, and the rope of the gunas that binds us so firmly to maya has been cut, can the seeker hope to experience oneness with the supreme Reality.

[1] The brahmin continued,

"The true source of misery
Is the acquisition of anything
That you hold dear.
One who knows this
And desires nothing
Will enjoy lasting happiness.

[2] "I once watched an osprey ~
Carrying flesh in its beak,
It was harassed by a bigger
And more powerful osprey.

Only after it had dropped the flesh
Was it again left in peace.

3 "I feel neither honor nor dishonor.
I do not care for the things,
Like houses and families and children,
That most people care for.
I wander through this world
As unburdened as an infant,
Rejoicing only in the Self.

4 "Only two beings in this world
Are free from all anxieties:
The infant who knows nothing
And the sage who knows the Self
Which is beyond the three gunas.

5 "Once, a maiden whose family were away
Had herself to receive the guests
Who had come to her home
To request her hand in marriage.

6 "She retired to the kitchen to prepare a meal.
As she pounded the rice
The shell bracelets around her wrist
Kept jingling loudly.

7 "Already ashamed to be greeting her guests alone,
This sensitive girl became even more embarrassed
By the sound of her bracelets as she worked.
So she removed them one by one,
Leaving only two on each wrist.

8 "But even these two bracelets on each wrist
Produced a sound.
So she removed a further two,
Leaving only one bracelet on each wrist.

9 "I learned this lesson from her, O king,
As I wandered through the world
Seeking to understand the ways of people:

¹⁰ "Where many people live together
They become quarrelsome.
Even when just two people live together,
They will chatter.
Therefore one should go alone through this life,
As silent as the single bracelet
On the maiden's wrist.

¹¹ "Holding a steady posture
One should quiet the mind
And control the breath.
Through the power of one's renunciation
And regular practice
This quiet will be sustained.

¹² "Then center the mind on the Self,
And slowly it will cease its activity:
Both rajas and tamas
Will be submerged into sattva.

¹³ "Like the arrow-maker
Whose mind was so centered on his work
That he did not even notice
The king passing by with loud fanfare,
So the Yogi must sit,
Not distracted by inner or outer activity.

¹⁴ "The sage should wander alone ~
Ever homeless and resorting to caves for shelter,
Ever aware.
Do not declare yourself a sage:
Let your silence be your hallmark.

¹⁵ "Be like the snake
That inhabits the hole
Others have dug and left.
Do not build a house,
For your body is perishable.

¹⁶ "At the end of each creation cycle,
The Supreme One, Narayana,
Withdraws this creation

And all its multiplicities.
Then the many
Once again return
To being the undifferentiated One
Without a second.¹

¹⁷ "Through the power of time,
Which is yet another manifestation
Of that supreme Controller,
The gunas then merge in the Absolute
In perfect equilibrium.

¹⁸ "Then only that Supreme Being remains.
The ancient one,
The god of gods,
The pure and unblemished,
The transcendent,
The One without a second ~
That alone remains.

¹⁹ "The One, through the power of time,
Begins the next creation cycle
By summoning the primordial vitality.
Through maya
This vitality rouses the gunas,
Calling into being a world
Which appears to be
Made up of multiplicities.

²⁰ "The great sages have said
That this primordial vitality
Manifests as the gunas,
Which account for the whole of creation
And each individual's
Birth, death and rebirth.

²¹ "Just as a spider
Sends forth a web from its heart
Out through its mouth,
And then draws it back into the heart,

So the One sends forth this world of multiplicity
And then draws it back into Itself.

22 "Whatever an embodied being centers the mind on,
Be it through love or hate or fear,
That we become.

23 "This is like the insect of legend
That was captured by the wasp:
He fixed his mind so intently on his captor
That he assumed the shape of the wasp.

24 "Thus I have learned from all these, my teachers.
Now listen, O king, and I will tell you
What I have learned
From my very own body.

25 "This body, which is subject to birth and death
And a source of great afflictions,
Has been a great teacher:
It has promoted my dispassion
And fuelled my self-enquiry.
It has brought me to the gates of reality.
This is because I realized
That not even this body
Can be called my own.
In truth, it belongs to those
That will devour it upon death.

26 "This body, for which people work endlessly,
Drawing to it spouse, children, wealth and home,
This body dies just as a tree dies ~
Leaving the seeds for the next birth.

27 "During a lifetime
The tongue will send you in one direction,
And your thirst in another;
The sexual impulse will lead you to one person
And the sense of touch to another.
Then the stomach, the ear and the nose,
The restless eye and your activities
Will seek to take you somewhere else.

All these will tear you to pieces ~
Like a husband with many wives.

28 "The ultimate Reality,
Through its own power,
Evolved many forms ~
Trees, snakes, beasts and insects,
Along with birds and fish.
But the human body
Is the ultimate creation,
For within the heart of the human form
Is the yearning to know
Its own true nature.

29 "Thus the wise,
Having attained a human body
After myriad births and deaths,
Seek to know the Self.
No matter how frail the body may be
It is still the means
Of attaining that final liberation.

30 "Thus having freed myself from attachment,
And possessing the light of that supreme knowledge,
I roam this world
Identifying completely with the Self.

31 "Although the truth is One,
For this knowledge to become constant
Many teachers are needed.
For the truth is imparted differently
By different sages."

32 The Radiant One, Krishna, said,

Having thus addressed the great king,
The young brahmin took his leave
And went on his way.

33 Listening to the teaching of this avadhuta,
The king, our ancestor, was freed from all attachment
And gained peace of mind.

❋ Dialogue 5

In Dialogue 5, Krishna's teaching suddenly becomes much more direct ~ stripped bare of stories it has the power to shake us to the core. Krishna tells us that we can continue to live with shadows of the truth, if that is what we wish. We can continue to commit ourselves to a body and personality that have no permanence ~ but then we have to deal with the consequence: staying on the wheel of birth, death and rebirth until we realize who and what we are. This is hard to swallow because we are so engaged by who we think we are. Yet it is obvious, if we stop to consider, that who we think we are is a social construct created by our family, friends, upbringing, education and social milieu. Each day we wake up and reconstitute ourselves around a construct that others have made. We accept the self that is forced on us before we have the good sense to know otherwise.

Whether we choose to believe in the theory of reincarnation or in the absolute authority of the gene, it is clear that we come into this world an "I" already in the making. The ancient texts refer to vasanas, which has the same root as the Sanskrit word for color. Vasanas are the impressions and "colors" present at birth, which, through memory and gene, blend with the life of the present. From birth, our awareness is entirely absorbed by this construct, which believes itself to be "I" but which is in reality an idea ~ and not even our own idea.

Three Sanskrit words are introduced here: yama, niyama and guru. Yama and niyama are not only values to be upheld, but truths to be discovered. Yama here means "restraint." Five "restraints" constitute our contract with society as seekers on a spiritual path. They are ahimsa, non-violence; satya, truthfulness; asteya, non-stealing; brahmacharya, living as a seeker of Brahman; and aparigraha, non-covetousness. Niyama are the contracts we make with ourselves: saucha, purity; santosha, contentment; tapas, regular practice; svadhyaya, study of truth; and Ishvara pranidhana, aligning with the Infinite.

The word guru means more than "someone who is an adept or a teacher," as it has become popularly applied. The guru is someone who removes the darkness of ignorance. Only someone who has themselves experienced the Infinite can do that.

¹ The Radiant One, Krishna, said,

Take refuge in me, dear friend,
And live your life in devoted service,
Performing all those duties¹ that are necessary
And fulfilling the purpose for which you were born.

² With your mind thus refined
Observe those who live their lives
Committed only to this world of objects ~
And the miseries that befall them.

³ Just as the images in a dream
Or a reverie are unreal,
So are the multiplicities
Of this world.
They come and go
Bound by the rope of the gunas.

⁴ Those who perform their duties
Devoted to the Self,
Rather than seeking
A reward for their actions,
Live a full life.
Live like them, Uddhava,
Refraining even from those rituals
That promise a reward.

⁵ One who is devoted to the Self
Should always attend to the yamas,
And to the appropriate niyamas.
Such a one should serve the guru
Who is of tranquil mind
And fully absorbed in the Self.

⁶ Such a devotee
Must be free from pride and jealousy,
Strong in devotion
And free from attachments.
Be completely devoted to the guru,
Prepared to perform all actions carefully,

Refrain from unnecessary chatter
And hunger only after the Truth.

7 All people and things must become equal
In the eyes of such a devotee ~
Be they spouse, children, home or wealth,
Friends or relatives.
The devotee must seek only the Self in all.

8 The Self, that self-illuminated consciousness,
Is separate from form,
As a fire which lights up the darkness
Is separate from the burning log.

9 Just as the fire burning a log
May appear as an ember,
A weak flame or a conflagration,
Depending on the state of the wood,
So the Self appears to assume
The attributes of the form it enters.

10 Identification with the body,
Which is created by the Supreme
Through the mysterious power of maya,
Is the cause of human bondage
To birth and death and rebirth.
Only knowledge of the Self
Can release one from that bondage.

11 Therefore, step by step,
Detach yourself from
Identification with the body:
Let your attachment be
Identification with the indwelling Self.

12 The guru is like the kindling
At the base of a fire,
The student is the wood placed on top ~
The teaching is what connects them:
Together they produce the spark
That lights the fire of knowledge
Which brings true joy to all.

13 The pure wisdom that comes
From the teaching of the guru
Removes the maya
Which binds the seeker
Through the power of the gunas.
When even that knowledge itself
Is burned like a fire with no fuel,
Only the Self remains.[2]

14 Now, if you continue to believe
That the multiplicity of forms,
The diversity of activities
And those engaged in them
For the sake of momentary pleasure,
Within a defined time and space,
Are the sole reality;

15 Or that performing the duties
Which the scriptures require
Will lead to the perpetuation
Of the individual soul,
Or bring some earthly benefits
In this world of objects,[3]

16 Then, my dear friend,
You will remain bound to this cycle
Of birth, disease, death and rebirth.

17 O Uddhava, it must be clear to you
That even one who works diligently,
Taking great care to try to control
The vagaries of life,
Is still subject to pain and pleasure.
What happiness can there be
In this kind of dependence?

18 Sometimes even intelligent people
Are caught in great misery,
While the fool seems untroubled.
To think that through diligent labor

You will avoid pain
Is a silly fantasy.

19 Even if a few people discover the means
To avoid unhappiness and disease,
They certainly never find a way
To stave off death.

20 When death is near
What wealth or pleasure can bring joy?
What can you offer someone
Who is being led to the gallows
That will bring pleasure?

21 What of heaven, you may ask.
I tell you, dear one, heavenly pleasures
Are the same as earthly ones ~
Contaminated by envy and rivalry,
Decay and waste.
Working towards a sojourn in heaven
Can be as uncertain as planting a crop
That may or may not grow.

22 But, for those who choose heaven,
Let me tell you of the path,
Because without clear guidance
It is almost impossible.

23 One who performs rituals
And worships the gods
In accordance with scriptural injunctions
Will go to heaven
And there enjoy heavenly pleasures.

24 These activities will be the vehicle
By which a person ascends
To the heavenly spheres ~
To be decked out in beautiful attire,
To eat, drink and be merry,
And have their praises sung by the ancestors.

25 There, enjoying all that heaven offers,
Every pleasure laid out before one,
Happy in the gardens of the gods,
Time will fly by
With no thought of the impending fall.

26 Then the terrible moment comes,
When all the merit earned by deeds
Done during the previous lifetime
Is exhausted.
Once again
That being falls down
Into embodiment,
Helplessly propelled by time.

27 On the other hand,
If one lives a life
Devoted to greed and materialism,
To fulfilling one's desires
Without a care for others,
Even causing them harm
In order to get one's way,
Associating only with those like oneself;

28 Or if one needlessly slaughters animals
Or engages in spirit worship,
Then one descends
Into various dark hells.

29 When such people
Again return to embodiment
They will continue to act in darkness ~
In which there is no possibility of happiness.

30 In all the spheres of existence
From the lowest to the highest,
Beings must fear time.
Even Brahma the creator,
Destined to be of unimaginable longevity,
Must cease to be when his time is up.

³¹ As long as beings are bound by the gunas,
They will see a world of distinctions and multiplicities
In which they identify only with their own
Individual body and personality.
And as long as they are bound in this way,
Every action they take will have a consequence.

³² As long as the gunas prevail
The individual is prey to fear
Born of taking form again and again.
In this state each person is bound
To the consequences of their actions.

³³ Those who are committed
To what they can see,
Hear, touch, taste or feel,
Are absorbed by the material world
And destined to live a life
Plagued by constant apprehension.

³⁴ Only the wise know
That what is called
The individual, or time, or the scriptures,
Or even the heavenly spheres,
All of that
Is the undivided and complete Self
Under the sway of the disturbed gunas.

³⁵ The devotee Uddhava asked,

Beloved, as long as the individual
Is bound to the body
Then she or he is surely also bound
To the actions and their consequences
That are the natural result of the gunas.
How is it possible to be embodied
And yet not bound?
If we say that the individual
Is forever transcendent,
And though embodied

Has nothing to do with the material world,
How do we come to be bound?

36 How do those who are not bound
And are yet embodied act?
What do they eat?
How do they sit?
How do they rest?
By what mannerisms can we recognize them?

37 O Teacher of Teachers,
Sometimes living beings are described
As eternally conditioned and bound.
At other times we are described
As eternally liberated and free.
Which is true?
Please clear my confusion.

❋ *Dialogue 6*

Krishna begins this dialogue by defining bondage and liberation; astonishingly, he states that neither is real. In the preceding dialogues, Krishna has prepared us to hear his core message and now, while our minds are still open in reaction to the statement that bondage and liberation are illusions, he points to the fundamental truth: that we do not know who we are. What we identify as ourselves is not Reality but a mere shadow of it ~ as Krishna puts it, a broken reflection on moving waters. All our pain, grief and suffering lie in that fragmented reflection, and not in the Reality that is being reflected. And it is our commitment to the reflection that constitutes our bondage.

Krishna ends the discourse by encouraging Uddhava to seek the Self through devotion, which he clearly sees as the right path at the dark dawn of the Kali Yuga, when Reality is becoming even more obscured. Perhaps, in this Kali Yuga, it is deep in the cave of the heart that we must retreat in order to find the Self. In retreating inward we are not defeated; rather we discover that we are more than we ever thought we could be. In that retreat lies true victory.

Dialogue 6 gives an inspiring description of a wise person. If the preceding text made one believe that a sage is unbearably aloof and remote, this dialogue will dispel that misunderstanding.

[1] The Radiant One, Krishna, said,

Neither bondage nor liberation is real.
Subject to the gunas ~ the three boundaries of nature,
The mind thinks of itself now as bound, now as free.
But since these boundaries are themselves illusory
I tell you, there is neither bondage nor liberation.

[2] At night when one is asleep
And the mind reflects upon the day,
We call this a dream.
Likewise grief and joy,
Living and dying and being born again ~
All are but a dream.

[3] O Uddhava,
Know that both knowledge and ignorance
Emanate from the Indweller, the Self of all ~
The one Reality.
Knowledge and ignorance
Are the cause of both freedom and bondage.
Knowledge, the source of freedom,
And ignorance, the source of bondage,
Have always existed
As a part of creation.

[4] You are wise, Uddhava, think now!
The individual soul is part
Of the one Reality.
Bondage is based on ignorance and
Liberation is based on knowledge
Of the one Reality behind the parts.[1]

[5] That which is free in you
And that which is bound
Have different qualities ~
Even though they occupy the same body.
Let me explain:

[6] The individual can be likened
To two birds,
Companions who nest in the same tree.
One eats the fruit of the tree,
The other refrains from eating.
Yet it is the one that does not eat
That is the source of strength for both.

[7] The Reality is like the bird that does not eat ~
It is enlightened:
It knows itself and it knows its companion.
The unreal is like the bird that eats ~
It is ignorant:
It knows neither itself nor its companion.
Only that bird filled by knowledge of the Self is free.

8 Just so are the wise ~
They have awakened from the dream.
And just as on awakening
You would not cling to a dream,
They do not cling to the body.
But ah! the ignorant ~
They still live in the dream.

9 The wise,
Though still of the body,
Are no longer confined to it.
The wise do not identify
With the things of the dream.

10 Those still trapped in the dream
Are caught by the mind reflecting on the past.
They are like the mind of the dreamer
That continues reflecting on the events of sleep,
And is bound to the things of dreams.

11 The wise become like the sky,
Like the sun,
Like the wind ~ free and unbound.
They can sit and walk, bathe and eat,
Hear, touch and smell:
Yet in the midst of all this living
The wise remain unbound by the gunas.

12 Living amidst all the objects of life
The wise person identifies
Solely with the unbound, undivided Self.

13 The body of the wise one
Remains tied to the boundaries of nature.
But ah! the wise understand the truth behind
The world of duality and multiplicity.

14 The wise live a spontaneous life
Free from the need for scheming and planning.
With energy, mind and intellect
Focused on the one Reality that encompasses all,
The wise are transparent.

¹⁵ Even when the body is cruelly tortured
By the pitiless ignorant,
Or by others worshiped,
The wise remain unaffected.

¹⁶ Viewing the ignorant torturer
And the admiring worshiper
With the same impartial vision,
The wise lay neither blame nor praise.

¹⁷ The wise
Will not think or speak of evil,
But will roam the world
With a mind fixed on the Self.

¹⁸ Be warned, Uddhava,
If someone is well versed in the scriptures
But does not have knowledge of the Self,
Then that one is not wise.
Indeed, that one can be likened
To a man who tends a cow that yields no milk.²

¹⁹ My dear friend, know also that
Anyone who maintains an unyielding cow,
Or an unfaithful spouse,
Or a body dependent on the labors of another,
Or an ungrateful child,
Or wealth that is not bestowed on the deserving,
And whose speech is devoid of the Self,
Such a one can know only misery.

²⁰ Dear Uddhava,
The wise enjoy speaking of the Self.
They delight in recounting the emergence of the Self
Through stories of creation and avatars.

²¹ Having cast aside the mistaken idea of multiplicity,
Their minds dwell on the one Self of all.
They do not think of acting this way or that
To please the world.
They think only of the indwelling Self of all.

22 Old friend,
If you are unable
To hold your own mind steadily on the Self
There are other ways of achieving wisdom:
Uncaring of the outcome for yourself,
Offer all that you do each day
To the one ineffable Self.[3]

23 Listen to stories and songs
About avatars like myself ~
These bring purity.
Imitate my deeds.
Take refuge in me.

24 Pursue your daily activities
And religious rites if you must,
But pursue them for the sake of the Indweller of all.
In this way your faith in the one eternal Self will grow.

25 Keep the company of saints and sages:
Such association draws one closer to the Self of all.

26 The devotee Uddhava asked,

Radiant One, Krishna, whom do you consider to be a sage?
And what kind of devotional practices
Do you consider to be best?

27 Indweller of all,
Whose presence spans the heavens,
Ruler of the universe,
Answer me
Who has prostrated himself before you,
And been devoted to you.

28 You are the One Reality ~
Expansive as the sky.
You are the supreme Self of all.
Yet you incarnated here as Krishna ~
Not through any past actions,
But by the power of your own will.

[29] The Radiant One, Krishna, replied,

I will tell you who is a sage:
One who is compassionate to all beings,
Who harms none,
Who is forbearing,
And whose strength is truthfulness.
One who is free from envy,
Whose mind is poised in both joy and sorrow,
And who seeks first and foremost the welfare of all.

[30] A sage's mind is not clouded by desires;
Rather it remains undisturbed
And in control of the senses.
Without any harshness towards others,
The sage will always have a pleasing manner,
Free from possessiveness or worldly concerns.
The sage will eat only to appease hunger
And will always fulfill whatever duty presents itself.

[31] A sage's judgments will be well considered
And not be hasty or superficial.
A sage will have overcome the six waves
Of cold, heat, greed, infatuation, hunger and thirst.
A sage will not seek honor,
Even while bestowing it on others.
Above all, the sage is given
To contemplation of the Self,
Even in times of adversity.
A sage will be friendly to all
And kind to those in misery.
A sage brings the light of knowledge
To all beings.

[32] One who renounces duty
Is also a sage.
But such renunciation must be done
With full understanding:
By renouncing the duties to which you are bound,
You forfeit their outcome ~ both good and bad.
One who can do this is a sage indeed.

33 But foremost of all
Sages are those who have faith,
Those who are devoted to the Self of all,
Even before they have experienced
The full knowledge of It.

34 They see the Self reflected
In all the objects of the world:
They worship It,
They touch It,
They praise It,
They speak of It.

35 Through such worship their faith grows ever stronger ~
And they begin to offer more and more of themselves
To the Self of all,
Surrendering themselves in service to that Self.

36 They recount the lives and deeds of avatars,
And observe sacred days.
They visit temples
And sing and dance their faith.

37 They discuss the scriptures with each other
And visit holy places.
These sages enjoy worship
And initiating others into worship of the Self.

38 They have a deep love
For that in which they see
The one Reality reflected.
They take joy in caring for
And keeping holy places and temples clean.

39 Busily sweeping,
Sprinkling scented water,
Creating mandalas:4
They are happy
As the servants of the temple.

40 To be such a sage
One must disregard fame,

One must refrain from haughtiness,
Pride and hypocrisy,
And not let others know of one's good deeds.
To be such a sage
One must not misuse the light of the lamp
Lit in honor of the one Reality.

41 To be such a sage
All that is dear to you
Must be offered to the one Reality.
Such an offering produces infinite results.

42 That Reality may be worshiped through many forms:
The sun, the fire and the milk-giving cow,
Also through the saint and the devotee.
Through water, earth and one's own body --
As through the bodies of all beings.

43 The Self in the sun is worshiped with Vedic chants.
The Self in the fire is worshiped with clarified butter.
The Self in the saint is worshiped through hospitality,
And in the milk-giving cow through fresh green grass.

44 Uddhava, worship the Self in the devotee
Through proper relations that flow from the heart.
Worship the sky through meditation.
Worship the waters of the earth with water.
And worship the Self in the air
By honoring the life-giving vitality
That permeates the whole of this creation.

45 Worship the Self in the earth with mantras[5]
To keep in mind that it is sacred ground.
Worship the Self in your body
Through the food you feed it,
And worship the Self in all
Through equal, unbiased vision.

46 Place an image of the Self on consecrated ground
And worship it.
Let this image be benign and loving,
And give it your full attention.

47 One who worships me in this manner,
With a carefully focused mind
And an abundant heart,
Reaches a state of flawless devotion.

48 Uddhava, my dear friend and counsel,
There is no more straightforward road to the Self
Than this path of devotion.
Come through me.
Be devoted to me.
I am the resort of the righteous.

49 Let me impart one more thing to you, Uddhava,
It is a secret which deserves to be guarded.
I tell it to you now before I leave,
For you have ever been
My faithful friend and companion.

✳ *Dialogue 7*

This is the one of the shortest yet also one of the most mystical of all the dialogues. It begins with Krishna speaking about satsanga, which means "keeping company with the wise and enlightened." Satsanga, he tells Uddhava, is the easiest way to control the mind and arrive at that state of ecstasy in which individual consciousness is merged with Infinite Consciousness. Krishna is emphatic that not even the path of sannyasa can lead to enlightenment as quickly as satsanga.

Why should this be? The background chatter that fills the mind is usually drawn from our social conversations. If we are constantly in the presence of those whose aim is to connect with the Infinite, or who have already touched it, then that will fill our mind and make it easier to bring under control. Krishna does not urge us to neglect our other practices; he simply points out that without satsanga they will be much less potent.

When Uddhava voices his confusion, Krishna replies with an extraordinary description of the ways in which we are individuals within creation while still being part of the one whole. The imagery this enumeration creates in the mind has a powerful impact on meditation.

[1] The Radiant One, Krishna, said,

Hear me, O Uddhava,
As I tell you the secret
Of spiritual enlightenment.
Neither Yoga nor Samkhya,
Nor dharma, nor the recitation of scriptures,
Nor sannyasa,[1] nor valuable social works,
Nor even charitable acts;

[2] Not vows of fasting,
Nor acts of ritual worship,
Nor repetition of mystical mantras,
Nor arduous pilgrimages,
Nor upholding the yama and the niyama
Will bring your mind under control

As quickly as
Association with the wise.

3 Such satsanga, O Uddhava,
Has been the elevation
And enlightenment of many.
Let me tell of them:
The gandharvas ~ celestial musicians,
The nagas ~ serpent demons,
The siddhas ~ perfected ones,
The guhyakas ~ secret ones,
And many others ~

4 The sons of Diti, mother of the anti-gods,
The Yatudhanas, the magicians and sorcerers,
Among humans ~
Those engaged in commerce,
Ordinary laborers,
Women,
Rogues,
And even those bound by passion and ignorance.

5 In each and every age
Satsanga is the supreme means of salvation.
Even Prahlada[2] ~ whose mother was Kayadhu,
Whom the sage instructed while she was with child ~
Attained enlightenment through satsanga
While still in the womb.

6 Vibhasana[3], the brother of Ravana,
Sugriva, the monkey king,
Hanuman, the exemplar of devotion,
Jambavan, the bear,
Gajendra, the elephant devotee,
Jatayu, the vulture,
Tuladhara, the merchant,
Dharmavyadha, the hunter,
Kubja, the hunch-backed maiden,
The gopis who tended the cows
And kept me company in childhood,

The wives of the brahmins of Vrindavana,
And countless others ~

7 None of these studied the scriptures,
And they never served the great saints,
Or observed any vows or austerities.
Yet through their association with me
Or with saints, sages and my devotees,
They attained liberation.

8 The gopis who tended the cows,
Even the cows, antelopes, serpents and trees,
All reached ecstatic union with the One
Through satsanga.

9 That is difficult to attain,
Even through the discipline of Yoga
And the study of Samkhya,
Through sacrificial rituals
And austerities,
Through charity
Or even through sannyasa.

10 When I was taken away from Vrindavana
With my brother Balarama,
The gopis, because of their love for me,
Were bereft of joy.

11 The days and nights with me in Vrindavana
Passed like moments,
But the days and nights of my absence
Seemed like years.

12 With their minds fixed on me,
With all their thoughts revolving around me,
They were no longer conscious of relatives and friends,
They were not even aware of their own bodies,
Much less of this world or the next ~
Like Yogis in a deeply meditative state,
They merged their consciousness with mine,
Just as the waters of many rivers merge with the ocean.

13 These were women uneducated in scriptural law,
They did not know my true nature or their own.
They simply desired my presence ~
They longed for me as their beloved.
Yet through the power of satsanga with me
They attained that state of consciousness
In which they merged with the supreme Brahman.

14 You should do likewise, beloved Uddhava.
Give up all injunctions and prohibitions,
All that you have heard or may hear
Related to scriptural do's and don'ts.

15 And take shelter in your heart;
There seek the Self.
Do this with complete devotion
And freed from all fear
You too will surely merge with me.

16 The devotee Uddhava said,

Beloved Master of Yoga,
I hear your words
But doubts still cloud my mind;
I am still confused.

17 The Radiant One, Krishna, replied,

The supreme One
Reveals itself through a multiplicity of forms ~
Those not just of the earth but also of the heavenly spheres.
It is within each form,
As the prana[4] that flows through sushumna nadi[5]
In which are situated the sacred chakras.
Its most gross manifestation
Is in muladhara chakra,
And its most subtle is in the life-breath.
It resides in anahata chakra,
The space of the heart,
Where it is the subtle, celestial sound
And the parts of speech.

18 Just as fire exists in a potential state in wood,
And manifests as a spark when friction is applied,
Which becomes a fire in the presence of air,
And a conflagration if oblations are poured on to it,
Likewise the Self manifests by degrees,
Even through the sounds that are uttered.

19 And not just through speech,
But also through the actions taken
By the hands;
Through taste and smell,
Touch and sight;
Through hearing and thinking
And self-awareness:
The Self is manifest through all of these.

20 The supreme unmanifest One
Is the life of all that is manifest
Through the power of its gunas
And through the power of time:
Like seeds planted in fields,
These become an entire creation.
But know this to be the truth:
It is the supreme undifferentiated One
That is the source,
The heart lotus of this universe.

21 The One is the warp and weft of creation.
All existence depends upon the One,
Just as the existence of the cloth
Rests on its woven threads.
This tree of samsara⁶ is ancient;
As it moves it sends forth fruit and flowers.

22 Good and bad deeds are its seeds;
Its hundreds of deep roots are desires;
Rajas, tamas and sattva are its support;
And the panchatattva: earth, water, fire, air and space
Are its five sturdy branches
Yielding five different kinds of sap ~

Smell, taste, sight, touch and hearing.
These five sturdy branches produce ten others
Which are called the indriyas, the organs of action ~
The nose, tongue, eyes, ears, skin,
The throat, hands, feet, anus, sexual organs,
Plus the mind.
Hidden in its branches
It carries the nests of two birds ~
The supreme One and the ahamkara, the idea-of-"I."
Its three layers of bark
Are the three humors of the body ~
Wind, bile and phlegm.
And it bears two fruits ~
Joy and sorrow.
This tree extends farther than the sun.

23 Filled with desires,
Some people, like vultures,
Will ravish the fruit of sorrow;
While those on the path of renunciation,
Living like swans in the forest,
Will eat of the fruit of joy.
One who truly understands the Vedas
And who has gained wisdom through the guru,
Knows that this tree is the supreme One,
Which grows through the power of the gunas
And the maya which the One has woven.

24 Now, Uddhava, this is my instruction to you:
With a quiet and watchful mind,
Sharpened by service to your guru,
Take up the axe of awareness
And cut this tree down.
Thus free the Self
And remain totally identified with the Self ~
Only then may you lay down your axe.

❋ Dialogue 8

In this dialogue, Krishna teaches about how to liberate oneself from the bondage of ignorance. He makes it clear that purity, passion and ignorance are states of the body and personality, and not of the indwelling Self. Again we are asked to question what it is that we identify as ourselves. Krishna tells the seemingly simple story of his appearance as a swan before sage Sanaka and the creator deity, Brahma. In answering their question, "Who are you?," Krishna leads us far beyond our conception of ourselves. Evolving in a connected and ultimately whole field of Reality, we emerge and cloak that Reality in flesh and bone, seeking to confine it to the ahamkara, the idea-of-"I." Each cell in our bodies, catalyzed by cascades of chemicals and neuronal signals, participates in concealing the truth, until we actively seek it out. Returning to a realization of Reality is the ultimate destiny of the human journey. To begin this journey the question must arise: if I am not who I think I am, then who am I?

Krishna always points us back to this instruction: look within ~ where all the wonder of Reality lies. But that requires moving beyond what psychologists call our "pre-cognitive commitments": those commitments we made to being the person we are, before we were even conscious we were making them.

[1] The Radiant One, Krishna, said,

The gunas belong to material nature
And material awareness
But not to the Self.
Through sattva,
Rajas and tamas may be overcome,
And then sattva,
In the shape of the virtues truthfulness and compassion,
Will overcome itself.

[2] In people who have developed sattva
Religious principles and devotion
Abide naturally.

These become strengthened
Through practice.

3 Sattva then becomes more powerful
And subdues rajas and tamas.
As these are eventually completely overcome,
All unrighteousness is destroyed.

4 Spiritual practices, water,
The people you associate with,
The time of day, season or year,
The activities you practice,
Your initiation into the spiritual way,
Your manner of contemplation,
The mantras you use for contemplation
And for chanting,
And your purificatory rituals
Are the ten contributors
To the predominance of any one guna.

5 Of these,
Whatever sages of sound judgment praise
Are sattvic in nature;
Whatever they condemn is tamasic;
And whatever they are indifferent to
Is rajasic.

6 To allow sattva to grow in oneself
One should nurture those things
That are sattvic in nature.
Only then will dharma become fixed
Within you.
From that proceed to Self-realization
In which you will once again know
Your own eternal and infinite nature.

7 Just like the fire
That springs up from dry bamboo
And rages through the forest,
So is the body
Born of the imbalance of the gunas.

But like the fire that has burned itself out,
So is the body:
On enlightenment it will cease to be.

8 The devotee Uddhava said,

We do know that seeking pleasure
Can lead only to pain.
So why do we constantly do it?
Are we no wiser than animals?

9 The Radiant One, Krishna, replied,

The idea-of-"I,"
Which is wholly related
To the body and personality,
Springs up in the mind of the deluded.
Then the quality of rajas
Overtakes the naturally sattvic state.

10 In the mind of a person
Under the influence of rajas,
All manner of desires will arise.
Each desire when focused on
Will in time become a burning passion.[1]

11 In the grip of these passions
And devoid of all self-control
The person will act in ways
That inevitably lead to sorrow.

12 The person who has begun
To set aside delusion and seek truth,
Does not yield to distraction
Though rajas and tamas rage within.
Such a person stays focused
On the quest for truth ~
Rather than rushing into folly.

13 Having learned how to hold a constant posture,
And having achieved control of the breath,
This person will sit three times a day
During the auspicious times

At dawn, noon and dusk,[2]
Quietly focusing the mind,
And practice concentration.

14 Withdrawing the attention
From the external world
The seeker fixes it on me.
This practice of Yoga
Was taught by me
To Sanaka and my other devotees,
The spiritual sons of Brahma, the creator.

15 The devotee Uddhava said,

Beloved Keshava,[3] please tell me,
When did you instruct Sanaka and the sages
In this science of Yoga?
I would dearly love to know it too.

16 The Radiant One, Krishna, said,

Sanaka and the other sages
Approach their spiritual father,
Brahma the creator,
And asked about the ultimate goal of Yoga,
Which is so difficult to achieve.

17 Sanaka spoke on behalf of the sages and said,

The mind is attracted to those objects
That it experiences through the senses.
The objects then begin to play upon the mind.
For one who wishes to go beyond
These ephemeral objects and attain enlightenment,
How does this process of acting and reacting cease?

18 The Radiant One, Krishna, said,

Being asked this question by the sages,
Brahma, the self-born creator of all things,
Thought deeply about the matter,
Which had at its root
Ignorance about the Self.
But his mind was too occupied

With the matter of creation
To come to the answer.

19 Brahma then fixed his mind on me
And as he did so I appeared there
In the form of Hamsa, the divine swan.4

20 Seeing me the sages all came forward
And prostrating, touched my feet.
Brahma, leading them, asked,
"Who are you?"

21 They were all eager to know the answer
To the question posed by Brahma.
Listen, O Uddhava,
To what I told them:

22 The question itself is confused.
If the question refers to the undivided
And imperishable Atman,5
Which is the Presence present everywhere,
How can I individuate myself to answer it?
If I try to answer,
What is it
That I can make distinct from that Presence
In order to answer?

23 However, if the question relates to the body,
Since all bodies ~ whatever their form ~
Are composites of the five tattvas
And are therefore in truth the same,
It still remains unanswerable ~
A mere affectation of speech.

24 Recognize this truth
With a clear understanding:
All the senses perceive only me.
I alone exist.
Nothing exists besides me.

25 You, who are being born again,
Must know that the mind

Is drawn to objects through the senses,
And in turn these objects influence the mind.
Thus both the body and the mind
Appear to cloak the Jiva:
But in reality both are the undivided Atman.

26 Therefore, cease to identify yourself with the mind,
Which is constantly drawn to objects through the senses,
And which then gets caught up in these objects.
Instead, identify yourself entirely
With that undivided Presence.

27 Waking, dreaming and sleeping
Are states of the body-mind
Functioning under the rule of the gunas.
They are not states of the Jiva,
Which is the eternal consciousness.

28 Material existence controlled by the gunas
Holds the Atman in bondage.
Transcend this bondage
By rising above the three states
Of waking, dreaming and deep sleep.
Enter the fourth state, turiya,
And liberate yourself.

29 Knowing that this bondage
Is solely due to the false identification
With body and personality,
Give it up.
Identify yourself with the immortal Atman
And be free.

30 As long as this world of multiplicity
Is real to you,
You are asleep even while you are awake ~
Like someone who imagines themselves awake
While they are dreaming.

31 All things that appear as multiplicity,
Not simply on this earth,
But even those that seem to belong

To the heavenly spheres ~
All are as unreal
As the objects seen by the dreamer
In a dream.

32 Awake, a person perceives a world
Filled with objects external to themselves.
Asleep, these objects are perceived
Within the person as a dream.
In deep sleep, the internal and external
Both disappear.
But through all these states
The Atman remains
The ever-conscious witness
And the continuity that connects them.

33 Look upon this world as an illusion ~
A transitory creation of the mind,
Here today and gone tomorrow.
In the grip of these three states of consciousness
Which are generated by the wildly fluctuating gunas.
Root out this idea-of-"I"
With the sword of wisdom
Sharpened by devotion
And worship of the saints.

34 See this world for what it is:
An illusion ~ no more substantial
Than a ring of fire
Traced by a burning torch in the dark;
An illusion colored by the gunas
And shaped as form.
In reality it is the one pure Consciousness
Which appears as the many.

35 Withdraw your attention from this world
With all its appearances of forms and objects.
Immerse yourself in the reality
Of that inner eternal bliss.
Be quiet and without ambition.
Then you will not be deluded

Even when you perceive your body
As separate and distinct,
Even though this impression
Remains until death.

36 One who is established in the Self
Does not give attention to the body,
Whether it is sitting, standing or walking,
Coming or going ~
Any more than the drunk
Gives attention to his attire.

37 The body and the prana
Will remain together
Until its destiny is complete.
To the Yogi who has attained samadhi
None of this is of any more concern
Than a dream.

38 O sages, I have given you the most secret
Instructions of both Yoga and Samkhya.
Know me to be Vishnu,
Come here to teach you dharma.

39 I am the supreme goal of Yoga and Samkhya.
I am all virtue and truth in practice and philosophy.
I am all glory and splendor.
I am that self-discipline which leads to the Self.

40 All the eternal virtues take rest and shelter in me.
All that is beyond the gunas lives in me.
I am free of all desires.
I am the most beloved friend of the Self.

41 With their doubts removed,
Sanaka and the other sages
Worshiped me with supreme devotion,
And sang my praises.

42 And as they and Brahma looked on
I returned to my own abode.

✳ Dialogue 9

In Dialogue 9, Krishna again encourages Uddhava to take the path of devotion. In the second half of the dialogue, he marks out this path with a beautiful and inspiring meditation that uses many of the techniques of Yoga and the concept of ishta devata.

The word ishta, derived from the Sanskrit root *is*, means "wish," and devata means "deity"; hence the meaning of the phrase is "wished-for deity" ~ the chosen deity that is worshiped in devotional practice. Krishna clearly offers himself as a possible ishta devata, though he does not say that only the form of Krishna, assumed in that particular time and space, can be used. When Krishna refers to "I," "me" and "mine" he means something very different from what we do. Remember his reply to Brahma and the sages when they asked, "Who are you?"

The Divine Presence cannot be confined to one form because it is all forms. It cannot be named because it is all names. It cannot be confined to one area of space because it exists everywhere, at all times. It is life, yet it existed before life began and will be there even after this universe collapses in on itself. Of this, Krishna ~ as the avatar, as the teacher of these scriptures ~ has a total awareness. However, in order to bring our minds under control, as these spiritual disciplines demand, we have to focus on something. As it is impossible for us to begin by focusing our minds on everything everywhere, we choose one thing ~ the ishta devata.

Krishna points out that the ishta devata is a means, not an end in itself. It is only after we have finished interacting with the multiplicities of the world that we can encounter the One. Ultimately, the ishta devata has to be dissolved so that the attention, free of images, sees the whole Reality, which before it saw only as fragments in a reflection. Only when the ishta devata is a means and not an end can the idea-of-"I" merge into the One. Thus Yoga is not about uniting two different entities but a realization that there was never any difference between them; as Krishna puts it in Verse 45, "fire uniting with fire."

Dialogue IX refers to the pranava mantra, Om. Om is the sound that is all sounds: all differences, all multiplicities gathered together to form the sound of the One. The pranava ("single-syllabled") mantra, Om is considered the most sacred of all sounds. The method for chanting Om that Krishna gives in this dialogue is uniquely effective in doing exactly what he promises ~ bringing the prana under control.

[1] The devotee Uddhava asked,

Teachers speak of different paths
Enumerated in the Vedas
That all lead to ultimate enlightenment.
Are all of them of equal value
Or is there one path of greater value?

[2] You have also described a path
That appears different from all the others ~
The path of devotion.
You seem to be saying that
Detaching the mind from the world
And attaching it to you
Is the golden way.

[3] The Radiant One, Krishna, replied,

During the last great dissolution of this creation,
My word, which gives humankind a way of conduct,
And which became known as the Vedas
Was completely destroyed.
At the beginning
Of the next cycle of creation
I again delivered it to Brahma.

[4] Brahma then gave this knowledge
To his eldest son, Svayambhuva Manu,
Who gave it to the seven great sages
Led by Bhrigu Muni.

[5] From the sons of Brahma the creator
Issued forth all the forms of creation ~
Including the demigods and demons,
The secret ones and humans,
The perfected ones and the celestial musicians,

Along with the bearers of wisdom
And those of good moral conduct;

6 Also all the humans that dwell on earth
And those that dwell in heaven,
Serpents and serpent demons,
The advanced species of monkeys,
And many other species of living beings.
All were the product
Of rajas, tamas and sattva.

7 All of the species
That people this universe,
Along with their leaders,
Appeared with different characteristics
And different tendencies.
Each according to their nature
Interpreted differently
This word of mine known as the Vedas.

8 People differ from each other
By nature,
Or by lineage,
Or by what they are taught.
Some are even atheists.

9 O Uddhava, best among men,
Because people are under the power of maya,
They will proclaim various paths as the best
According to their own nature and activities,

10 Some will advocate duty as the supreme way
And others religious activities.
Some will choose fame and sense-gratification
While others will be sure of the path of self-discipline.
Some will pursue the path of peace
And yet others the path of political power and influence.
Some will applaud grand, opulent living,
While others will preach renunciation.
Each path will have its own believers.

11 Each of these paths will have
A beginning and an end.
Each will bear the fruit
Of the actions taken on it.
But because each path will end
The outcome can only be sorrow.

12 Learned Uddhava, friend,
How can anyone attached to the objects
Of this world or the next
Know the bliss
Of one whose mind
Is fixed on me,
The blissful Self of all?

13 For the person who craves nothing,
Who sees all things with equal vision,
Who is content,
And whose mind rests
In that immortal bliss,
What more can there be?

14 Neither the abode of Brahma,
Creator of the universe,
Nor the heavenly spheres
Ruled by Indra,
Nor the mystical powers of the Yogi,
Hold any attraction
For one who has surrendered
The mind to me.

15 My dear friend Uddhava,
Neither Brahma, born of me,
Nor Shiva
Nor Shankarshana,[1] my own expansion,
Not even the goddess of fortune,
Nor my own self as a deity being worshiped,
Are as dear to me as you are,
You who are my devotee.

16 I always follow the footsteps
Of those who are devoted to me,
Who are without personal desire
And of even mind,
For the dust of their feet,
Will sanctify me.

17 These exalted souls,
Penniless and yet wanting nothing,
Blissful, calm and compassionate to all,
Whose minds have merged with me,
Only they can act without a thought for gain ~
Not others.

18 Even my devotee who has not yet
Mastered the senses
Will not be overcome by them
Because of that devotion.

19 Just as fire burns wood to ashes,
So does devotion to me
Burn all past transgressions.

20 Uddhava, neither Yoga nor Samkhya,
Nor piety nor austerities,
Are as uplifting as devotion
To that Self.

21 I, the Self of the righteous,
Am attainable through devotion alone.
Such devotion is the summit
Of a life of faith.
Such devotion can uplift
Even the most outcast of society.

22 Piety, truthfulness and compassion
Combined with learning and austerity
Will not purify a mind
Devoid of devotion.

23 Through the devotion of a softened heart,
Which brings tears of joy,
The mind is purified.

24 One who is devoted to me,
Who speaks of me in a voice
Filled with love,
Whose heart overflows with compassion,
Who weeps to think of being separate from me,
Who laughs at the joy
Of knowing I am within,
Such a one sanctifies this entire world.

25 Just as gold is smelted in fire
To remove the dross,
And then smelted again
To be made into form,
So is the Atman.
The first fire is that devotion
Known as Bhakti Yoga:
It removes all impurities
And returns the self to the Self.

26 Just like the eye that can better see
After an application of eye-lotion,
The more the mind is refined
By listening to tales of my glory,
The more it is able
To perceive and identify with the Self.

27 The mind of one who thinks
Of the objects of this world
Is attached to this world.
The mind of one who thinks
Of me only,
Merges with me only.

28 Therefore cease dwelling on unreal things
That have no more substance than a dream,
And with your mind purified by devotion
Focus on me.

[29] Give up association based on sensual pleasures
And the company of people
Committed to those pleasures.
Take your seat in a secluded and pleasant place
And remaining completely aware
Concentrate your mind on me.

[30] Association with others
Based solely on sensual pleasures
Can bring only misery.

[31] The devotee Uddhava asked,

Please tell me, O Lotus-eyed Beloved,
How should I meditate?
Should I use a form or an image?
Or should I meditate on the impersonal Self of all?
Tell me how to fix my mind on you.

[32] The Radiant One, Krishna, replied,

Sit in a comfortable posture, Uddhava,
In which your back, neck and head flow in a straight line
On even ground.
Place your hands, palms upward, on your lap
And direct your gaze downward.

[33] Withdraw your attention from the senses
By becoming aware of the breath.
First, fix your mind on the in-breath:
Breathe in slowly, hold the breath in,
Then breathe out slowly.
Fix your mind on that out-breath:
Breathe out slowly, hold the breath out,
Then breathe in again.

[34] Gradually let the prana
Flow up the shining pathway of sushumna,
As fine as a lotus stalk.
When it reaches the silence of anahata chakra
Let the sacred pranava mantra, Om,
Sound there ~ like the peel of a bell.

Then on the outbreath
Let that mantra flow from you.

35 Practice combining the breath in this manner
With the sacred pranava mantra, Om.
Do this ten times at each sitting
Three times a day.
In one month
You will have enough control of the prana
To embark on meditation.

36 Deep within the cave of the heart
There is a lotus in bud pointing downward.
Its center is enveloped by eight petals
And its stalk flows upward.

37 During meditation
Visualize this lotus turning upward
And its petals opening.
In its center see the sun, the moon and fire ~
All existing one within the other.
Then see the Self ~
In whichever form of mine you choose.[2]

38 Only let the form be beautiful beyond compare.
Let it be well proportioned and symmetrical,
Serene and benign.
Let it smile upon you and be gracious to you.

39 Look well upon my beloved form
In the center of the heart lotus.
I will be there:
The color of a dark rain-cloud,
Face and eyes shining with graciousness,
Tenderness flowing from me,
The goddess of fortune resting on my chest.

40 Picture me with ankle-bells and bracelets,
And radiant lotus-feet,
Bedecked with precious jewels
Brilliant and beautiful.

⁴¹ Slowly let this image build,
Encompassing all parts of my body.
Visualize my whole self
As being present there.

⁴² Keep withdrawing from all external objects
And fix your mind on that form
In the center of the heart-lotus,
Going inward, ever inward.

⁴³ Then, when the attention is flowing inward
In a continuous, unbroken stream,
Fix it on the benign face of the form only
And hold it there.

⁴⁴ Keep the attention steady.
Let the form evaporate and in its place ...
Behold the Self of all.
Ah! There behold That
Which is.
Let your whole being be absorbed by that Self.
Let that Self fill your entire being.
Let all distance
Between the Self of all and yourself
Be dissolved.

⁴⁵ Remain like that ~
Absorbed in the Self:
Like fire uniting with fire.

⁴⁶ One who can concentrate thus,
And achieve the focus required,
Is a Yogi.
For such a one,
Liberation from the world of multiplicities
Is near, very near.

In Dialogue 10 Krishna describes the siddhis. The word siddhi means "perfection" and refers to the mystical powers said to follow once perfection has been attained in various spiritual disciplines, particularly focused meditation.

I have a friend who has lived in a monastery, practicing different forms of Yoga and meditation, for some twenty-five years. A letter I received from her illustrates the idea of the "results" of focused meditation very well. She wrote, "Of course, I wonder sometimes if it's all worth it. But then there are the moments like last week, when I was stepping on to the bus and became aware that, probably for the first time in my life, all of me was going in the same direction."

When we attain this kind of wholeness new possibilities emerge, new abilities are at our disposal. Traditionally, these include being able to see the past, present and future; being able to choose one's moment of death; being able to become smaller than an atom. There is no need here to engage one's belief system; we may "believe" such possibilities exist or we may not. Krishna seems not to care. He simply enumerates them because, depending on the type of ishta devata you choose, powerful results called siddhis will accrue. However, like Patanjali, he ends by warning the seeker against actively seeking these powers. All things, Krishna says, come unsought to those who are devoted to Brahman. Actively seeking or engaging these powers, even when they come unsought, acts as a strong impediment to spiritual growth.

[1] The Radiant One, Krishna, said,

To the Yogi of balanced mind
Who is able to fix awareness on me,
Who has both the senses and the prana in control,
The siddhis will offer themselves.

[2] The devotee Uddhava asked,

You are the giver of all the siddhis.
Pray, tell me, how many are there?
What are they?
What does one have to do to receive them?

3 The Radiant One, Krishna, said,

Those that are masters of Yoga
Say there are eighteen siddhis in all.
Of these, eight are granted by me
And the remaining ten flow naturally
From the pure guna, sattva.

4 The eighteen siddhis are:
Anima, to become smaller than the atom;
Mahima, to become larger than the largest body;
Laghima, to become lighter than the lightest body;
These three siddhis pertain to the body.
The other siddhis are:
Praptih, to establish contact with the senses of creation;
Prakamyam shruta drishteshu,
To enjoy all that is seen and heard,
The visible and the invisible
That is found in the scriptures;
Ishita, to direct maya according to one's wish;

5 Vashita, non-attachment
To the pleasures of the senses;
Kamah avashayita, to enjoy the highest bliss;
These eight siddhis, O gentle Uddhava,
Are the primary siddhis and they flow from me.

6 The remaining siddhis are:
Anumi mattvam, the absence of hunger and thirst,
Disease, distress, old age and death;
Sravana darshanam, to hear and see from a distance;
Manah javah, to move the body
With the swiftness of the mind;
Kama rupam, to assume any form that is desired;
Parakaya pravesanam, to enter another's body;

7 Svachanda mrtyuh, to die
According to one's own will;
Sahakridanudarsanam, to participate
In the pastimes of the gods;
Yatha sankalpah samsiddhih,
To fulfill any wish or act of will;

Ajnapratihata gatih, to have one's will
Obeyed without objection.

8 Tri kala jnatvam, to know the past, present and future;
Advandvam, to be unaffected
By opposites like heat and cold,
Sorrow and joy, pain and pleasure;
Para citta abhijnata, to read others' thoughts;
Agnyarkambuvishadinam, to counteract the power
Of the sun, water, fire, poison and other threats;
Pratsihtambho aparajayah,
Not to be overcome by anyone.

9 The last five siddhis described
Come specifically from the focus
Developed through Yoga.
Now I will tell you
The specific siddhis that arise
From the different forms of meditation.

10 The siddhi anima is attained by the Yogi
Who meditates on me as the subtle element
That pervades everything, everywhere.

11 The siddhi mahima is attained by the Yogi
Who meditates on me as the Supreme tattva
Which absorbs each tattva ~
Earth, water, fire, wind, space.

12 The siddhi laghima is attained by the Yogi
Who meditates on me as that which empowers
The atoms of each of these Mahat Tattvas.

13 The siddhi praptih is attained by the Yogi
Who meditates on me as
That element which gives rise to the idea-of-"I"
Within all beings.

14 The siddhi prakamyam is attained by the Yogi
Who meditates on me as the supreme Atman,
The all-pervading thread of consciousness
Within all beings.

15 The siddhi ishita is attained by the Yogi
Who meditates on me as Vishnu,
The ruler of maya within all beings.

16 The siddhi vashita is attained by the Yogi
Who meditates on me as Narayana,
The fourth and transcendent phenomenon
Within all beings.

17 The siddhi kamah avashiyate is attained by the Yogi
Who meditates on me as Brahman,
The all-expansive being
Present everywhere and yet transcending everything.

18 The siddhi anumi mattvam is attained by the Yogi
Who meditates on me as Svetadvipa,
The embodiment of virtue.

19 The siddhi sravana darshanam is attained by the Yogi
Who meditates on me as the transcendent sound
Which vibrates through air and space;

20 And who meditates on me
As the sun that shines and the eye that sees
And the light of both.

21 The siddhi manah javah is attained by the Yogi
Who meditates on me as the unifying force
Of body, breath and the mind.

22 The siddhi kama rupam is attained by the Yogi
Who meditates on me as the form
That assumes all forms.

23 The siddhi parakaya pravesanam
Is attained by the Yogi
Who meditates on himself entering another's body
Through the pathway of prana ~
As easily as a bee enters and leaves a flower.

24 The siddhi svachanda mrtyuh
Is attained by the Yogi
Who has learned the art

Of blocking the anus with the heel,
And guiding the prana from the heart
To the spiritual seat at the crown of the head,
The place known as brahma randhrena,
And is then able to direct the prana
To whatever location she or he desires.

25 The siddhi sahakridanudarsanam
Is attained by the Yogi
Who has become aligned with my sattvic nature.
Then celestial nymphs, who are the product of sattva,
Will descend from their heavenly realms.

26 Yatha sankalpah samsiddhi is attained by the Yogi
Who has complete faith in me
And who knows that my will is always done.

27 The siddhi ajnapratihata gatih is attained by the Yogi
Who has merged with my self-contained Oneness
In which all things move.

28 The siddhi tri kala jnatvam is attained by the Yogi
Who has been purified by devotion to me
And knows perfectly the process of meditation.

29 The siddhi advandvam is attained by the Yogi
Whose mind has been completely calmed
Through Yoga practices and devotion to me.

30 The Yogi who meditates on me and all my glory ~
That devotee is unconquerable.

31 The sage who worships me in all the ways
Described here by me,
And who has perfected
The Yogic practice of dharana,
To that sage will flow
All the siddhis recounted here by me.

32 To the sage who has conquered the senses,
The breath and the mind,
Who is able through meditation

To become absorbed in me,
No siddhi is impossible to achieve.

33 But know this, O best among men:
Those who practice the best Yoga,
Which is to seek union with me;
Who are wise and wish to overcome maya,
They know that these siddhis are obstacles.

34 Know also that whatever siddhis can be achieved
By an auspicious moment of birth,
Secret herbs and mystical mantras,
Can be achieved only through devotion to me.

35 O Uddhava, I alone
Am the cause and the protector
Of all the siddhis.
I am the master of Yoga,
Religious rites and the teachers of the Vedas.

36 I am that supreme Self within all
And outside of all:
To all creatures,
The elements exist ~ internally and externally ~
I alone am enveloped by nothing.

We find a new Uddhava in this dialogue. Like any spiritual seeker, he has gone through a process. Uddhava began by begging Krishna not to leave him behind ~ a simple act of worship that lacked faith in his own mission in life. In Dialogue 11, he accepts his mission ~ his dharma.

Whenever I read these dialogues and witness Uddhava's progress ~ which represents the progress of everyone on a spiritual journey ~ I realize how inevitable that progress is. Whatever our inclinations, we begin by wishing to draw closer to a Divine that we see as existing outside of ourselves. Then, as that wish begins to shape our life, we see the Divine reflected in ourselves and in all material existence.

Enjoy the triumph of this dialogue as it allows us to begin to view the Divine with a human mind, though through the veil of the mind's perceptions. Yet, by contemplating the forms of the Divine that Krishna enumerates, the mind can move to a greater understanding of the reality of the world. Krishna allows us to "see" the embodied Divine through our bodily senses ~ as the stars, the planets, the creatures of the earth and sea, and so on. As Krishna, through the splendors of the world, makes the Divine actual for us, the quality of our experience of the world must change.

We have to proceed with caution, however. Just as no scientist, no matter how technologically sophisticated, expects to "see" a theoretical unit of matter such as a quark or a black hole, we will not "see" Brahman ~ the Reality ~ until we have gone beyond the limitations of individual perception. There is nothing more we can add to ourselves to see the Divine better. All we can do is look about and remind ourselves of what Krishna has said, that all this is the Self. Then, as we continue to walk the spiritual path, we will be stripped of everything that prevents us from experiencing that Presence directly.

[1] The devotee Uddhava said,

You, Beloved,
Are the beginning, the middle and the end.
You are the Supreme,
Unobscured and untouched by maya.

2 You are the great and the small,
The living and the non-living ~
That which those
Not devoted to the Self
Cannot understand,
And that which those
Dedicated to the search for truth
Can come to know.

3 Pray tell me, Beloved,
All the forms and ways
In which the wise
May contemplate you.

4 Originator of the Universe,
As the Self you are hidden within all.
We are not aware of you
Yet you are aware of us.

5 Tell me of all your manifestations:
The ways you have appeared among us
Invested with divine glory ~
On earth, in the heavenly realms
And in the dark hellish places.
Tell me, who prostrates before your lotus-feet,
The sanctuary of all.

6 The Radiant One, Krishna, said,

Your questions show insight, my friend.
You bring to mind that other dear one, Arjuna,
On the battlefield of Kurukshetra.[1]
Just before the battle was to commence
He too asked this question.

7 He was caught in a terrible war
Which he did not want to fight,
Feeling that to kill his kinsmen
To gain a kingdom
Was very wrong.
The error in his thinking was:

"I, Arjuna, will be the killer of my kinsmen.
And then they will all be dead."

8 I was able to inspire Arjuna,
That warrior of all warriors,
By showing him the flaw in his reasoning:

9 It is I, the Self of all,
Which disposes of life,
While cherishing all.
Beloved Uddhava,
I am all that is.

10 I am that which you
And all seekers seek.
I am motion in that which moves,
Among conquerors I am time.
In the gunas I am perfect balance.
In the good I am virtue.

11 In all that is manifest,
I am primary.
I am also
All that is unmanifest,
I am the most obvious
And I am the most subtle.
Among things difficult to conquer
I am the mind.

12 I am Hiranyagarbah,[2] the resplendent Self-Existent
From which Brahma emerged to teach the scriptures.
Among mantras I am the pranava mantra, Om.
Of the letters of the alphabet I am "a",[3] the beginning.
Among the sacred chants I am the three-lined Gayatri.[4]

13 Among the gods I am Indra.
Among the deities of the eight spheres I am Agni.[5]
Among the law-givers I am Vishnu.
Among the destroyers I am blue-throated Shiva.

14 Among the great seers I am Bhrigu.[6]
Among the royal seers I am Manu.

Among the divine seers I am Narada.
Among the sacred cows I am Kamadhenu,
The wish-fulfilling cow.

15 Among the perfected ones I am Kapila.7
Among birds I am the divine eagle, Garuda.
In the genesis of humankind I am Daksha.
Among the sainted forefathers I am Aryama.

16 O Uddhava, among the anti-gods
Know me to be Prahlada, king of kings.
Among those that worship
The finite and the demonic,
I am Kubera, wealth.
To the stars and herbs
I am the moon.

17 Among the stately elephants
I am Airavata,8 elephant of Indra.
Among the dwellers of the oceans
I am Varuna, lord of the seas.
Among shining objects,
I am the sun.
Among humans I am the sovereign.

18 Among steeds I am the steed of Indra.
Among metals I am pure gold.
Among those that rule death
I am Yama,9 lord of death.
Among serpents I am Vasuki, their chief.

19 Among the divine serpents I am
Anantadeva, god of them all.
Among beasts with sharp teeth
I am the lion.
Among the states of life I am sannyasa,
The final stage of renunciation.
Among social occupations I am a brahmin,
Teacher and priest.

20 Among the sacred flowing waters
I am the Ganga.
Among large bodies of water
I am the ocean.
Among weapons I am the bow.
Among warriors I am Shiva.

21 Of the Himalayas I am Mount Meru,[10]
The highest and most difficult to reach.
Among trees I am the sacred banyan.
Among grains I am barley.

22 Among priests I am Vashishta,[11]
Foremost of all priests.
Among those devoted to the Vedas
I am the most devoted, Brihaspati.
Among military generals
I am Kartikaya, most brilliant of all.
Among the greatest teachers of good
I am Brahma.

23 Of all the sacrificial rites
I am the daily recitation of the Vedas.
Among vows I am the vow of non-violence.
Among that which purifies
I am the wind, fire, sun, water and speech.

24 Among the eight limbs of Yoga
I am samadhi, the final state of liberation.
I am political astuteness in those that seek victory.
Among sciences I am that science
By which matter and spirit may be distinguished.
Among theologians I am faith.

25 Among women I am Satarupa,[12]
She of countless forms.
Among men I am her husband,
Svayambhuva, the self-born.
Among sages I am Narayana.
Among celibates
I am the supreme celibate, Sanatkumara.

26 Of religious virtues
I am renunciation.
Among sources of protection and well-being
I am meditation on the infinite Self.
Among the secretive
I am pleasant speech and I am silence.
Among couples I am Brahma ~
The first-born, the self-born,
Who became man and woman.

27 In the rhythm of time
I am the ever-revolving year.
Among the seasons
I am spring.
Of the months I am the most pleasant, Margarshirsha,13
Of the constellations I am the most auspicious, Abhijit.

28 Of the four ages
I am the Satya Yuga ~
The age of truth.
Among the self-controlled
I am the sages Asita and Devala.
Among the compilers of the Vedas
I am Dvaipayana.
Among the wise
I am the incomparable Shukra.

29 Among the radiant ones
I am Vasudeva.14
Among devotees
I am you, O Uddhava.
Among the half-divine
I am Hanuman.
Among the bearers of wisdom
I am Sudarshana.

30 Among precious stones
I am the red ruby.
Among beautiful things
I am the lotus.
Of all the grasses that grow

I am the sacred kusha[15] grass.
Of all the offerings
Thrown into the sacrificial fire
I am ghee.

31 Among the enterprising
I am riches.
Among the fraudulent
I am the gambler.
Among the tolerant
I am forbearance.
Among the good
I am goodness.

32 Among the strong
I am strength of body
And strength of mind.
I am the devotional practices
Of the devotee.
Of the nine forms worshiped
I am the foremost, Vasudeva.

33 Among the celestial singers
I am Vishvavasu.
Among the celestial nymphs
I am Purvachitti.
I am the firmness of mountains
And I am the fragrance of earth.

34 In water I am sweetness,
And among the glorious I am the sun.
I am the light of the sun, the moon and the stars.
I am the transcendent sound of space.

35 Among the worshipers of brahmins I am Bali
Who gave sovereignty of
Heaven, earth and his own body
To one whom he thought was a brahmin.
Among the valiant I am Arjuna.
I am the genesis, existence and dissolution
Of everything ever created.

36 In the living I am movement,
Speech, rejection, acceptance,
Enjoyment, touch and sight,
Taste, hearing and smell.
I am that power
By which
The senses enjoy
The objects of this world.

37 I am the supreme Self of the living.
I am the ahamkara, the idea-of-"I,"
And I am the transcendent I.
I am the elements of creation
And I am the field of consciousness.
I am all that I have stated I am.
Those of steady mind
Know the truth of this,
And know that I am this truth.

38 As the supreme Self
I am the Jiva of the living
And the Self that transcends the living.
Nothing exists that is not me.

39 Even though in time
I might enumerate the atoms of this universe,
My glory will never be enumerated
For it manifests through countless universes.

40 Wherever you find power, beauty or fame,
Grandeur, humility or renunciation,
Pleasure, wealth or strength,
Tolerance or spiritual knowledge;
Know these to be a manifestation
Of myself.

41 Now, Uddhava, I have told you
Of the forms that you may find me in.
Understand, dear friend, these are the forms
Perceived by the mind
According to its refinement.

42 Control your speech and
Discipline your mind.
Learn to master your vitality,
Regulate your senses
And refine your intellect.
By so doing
You will never again
Go through the cycle of birth, death and rebirth.

43 To the renunciate
Who has not controlled speech and mind
Through the power of will,
All austerities, vows and charitable works
Will become as nothing ~
Just as water seeps away
From an unfired pot,
Leaving the vessel empty.

44 Let your awareness be fixed on me.
Surrender mind, speech and prana to me.
Then you will attain your goal.

Dialogue 12 takes a new approach. In previous dialogues, Krishna has emphasized the need for renunciation. Uddhava now asks what those who do not live as renunciates can do. In reply, Krishna describes how the ancient varnashrama system, which encompasses caste and the stages of life from youth to old age, enabled individuals to live collectively in harmony with each other ~ and in the spirit of renunciation.

One of the tragedies of modern life, and one of the crises facing the urban, metropolitan person, is the individual's loss of purpose. From every corner the cry goes up: "What should I do with my life?" One of my teachers, Swami Agnivesh, founder of the Bonded Labor Liberation Front, believes that caste should be seen as the means for an individual to serve society. He says that the work of the brahmin should be to fight ignorance, that the work of the kshatriya should be to fight injustice, and that the work of the vaishya should be to fight poverty.

Communities have always sought ways of living together that allow individuals to express their strengths while protecting each other from their weaknesses. However, Swami Agnivesh is against the way the varnashrama system is currently practiced, in which caste is passed on by birth and used as a religious and cultural justification for social prejudice and economic exploitation. Rather, he says, we should all get to know ourselves well enough to understand our purpose in life, though this depends on every child being afforded the education that would allow her or him to make that kind of self-analysis. After such an education, if the young person still has not decided what to do, he or she could be apprenticed to someone of caste until they discover their own mission in life. Such apprenticeship would be known as the shudra caste. Swami Agnivesh's view of the varnashrama system perfectly reflects the teaching of Krishna in Dialogue 12.

[1] The devotee Uddhava said,

You have given us all,
Regardless of our place

In the varnashrama[1] system,
A way of upholding spiritual principles
Through devotional service to you.

[2] Now pray tell me,
O Lotus-eyed Prince,
How we may fulfill this devotion
While maintaining our own
Allotted duties according to the social order.

[3] O Mighty One,
In the form of a divine swan
You gave Brahma and the sages
An auspicious teaching
That will bring happiness to all.

[4] Now, Beloved,
That teaching which you gave
Has been lost to this mortal world.
Pray, teach it to us again.

[5] O Teacher of Teachers,
You pave and protect
The spiritual path.
Not even in the court of Brahma,
Where all the sciences are practiced,
Will we find such a teacher.

[6] O Slayer of the Demon Madhu,[2]
You are the creator, protector
And Supreme Teacher of the spiritual path
Known as dharma.
When you leave this earth
Who will be left to teach us?

[7] Therefore, most holy Beloved,
Knowing the dharma
In all its complexities,
Teach us.
Let us know who may practice it
And how it may be practiced.

⁸ Blessed Shuka resumed,

The Exalted One, Krishna,
Was highly pleased
With these questions
Posed by Uddhava.
He then taught
The time-honored teaching
Intended for all.

⁹ The Radiant One, Krishna, said,

Your question, my dear friend,
Is a good one.
Hear from me how all people,
Each observing their own duties
And following the varnashrama system,
May promote the highest good
For all.

¹⁰ In the very first age
Of this cycle of creation,
There was only one caste
Known as the hamsa caste
To which all people belonged.
Virtuous from birth,
Everyone had everything they needed,
And hence it was known as the Krita Yuga ~
The Age of Accomplishment.

¹¹ In that Krita Yuga
The pranava mantra, Om,
Alone was the scripture,
While dharma was as firm
As a bull standing
On all four legs.
People of that age
With one-pointed devotion
Worshiped me,
The Immaculate.

12 Blessed Uddhava,
In the following age,
Known as the Treta Yuga ~
The Age of the Three ~
Because this dharma, the bull,
Now stood on only three legs,
The scriptures known as the Vedas
Flowed from my heart
Borne by my exhalation.
These became the *Rig, Sama* and *Yajur Vedas*
And also the priests
Who perform the sacrificial ritual.

13 From the cosmic body of the Supreme
Came all people:
Those disposed to spiritual learning,
The priests who were to be called brahmins,
Sprang from the mouth of the Supreme.
Those ready to defend justice and truth,
The kings and princes
Who were to be called kshatriya,
Sprang from the arms of the Supreme.
Those who could bring prosperity and comfort
The farmers and merchants
Who were to be called vaishyas,
Sprang from the legs of the Supreme.
Those who wished only to serve humanity,
The servants and tillers of land
Who were to be called shudra,
Sprang from the feet of the Supreme.

14 The students living the life of celibacy
Devoted to learning,
Known as the brahmacharya stage of life,
Emerged from the heart of the Supreme.
Those who would follow a life
Of household, marriage and children ~
Known as grihastha,
Emerged from the loins of the Supreme.

The religious recluses of the forests ~
Who would live the vanaprashtha stage of life,
Emerged from the chest of the Supreme.
Those who would renounce all of this
And retire to a life of contemplation
Known as sannyasa,
They emerged
From the crown of the head of the Supreme.

15 The tendencies of the different castes
And the different stages of life,
All emerged from the different regions
Of the cosmic body of the Supreme.

16 Let me tell you what the tendencies of
A brahmin are:
To have control of the mind and the senses;
To be able to meditate;
To practice purity, contentment,
Compassion and truthfulness;
To be forbearing and straightforward;
And to be devoted to the Supreme.
All of these are characteristics
Of one who would be called a brahmin.

17 Let me tell you what the tendencies of
A kshatriya are:
To have dynamic strength
Both physically and spiritually;
To be courageous and tolerant,
Generous and steady,
Able to lead and able to serve.
All these are characteristics
Of one who would be called a kshatriya.

18 Let me tell you what the tendencies of
A vaishya are:
To have faith in the scriptures
And the teaching of the guru;
To be without deceit;
And never tire from increasing

The wealth of which he or she is the guardian.
All these are characteristics
Of one who would be called a vaishya.

19 Let me tell you what the tendencies of
A shudra are:
A guileless desire to attend to the needs
Of the initiated
And to care for the sacred cows
That yield the milk used for the oblations
Offered in sacrifice and as food;
Worship of the gods and of the guru
And contentment with that
Which is obtained from such service.
All these are characteristics
Of one who would be called a shudra.

20 Those who live outside a caste
Will tend towards a lack of faith.
They will become dishonest in their dealings ~
Stealing and quarreling needlessly.
Impurity, anger and desire
Will be the characteristics
Of those outside the varnashrama system.

21 Non-violence, truthfulness and honesty,
Freedom from desire, anger and greed,
Always seeking the happiness
And well-being of all ~
These are the hallmark
Of those inside the varnashrama system.

22 Whoever answers the summons
To enter the house of the guru[3]
For concentrated study of the scriptures,
And who undergoes the initiation rites
Through which they are reborn,
They are called the twice-born.

23 Such a brahmacharin studying with the guru
Should wear only a girdle of grass

And the skin of a deer.
Without attention to personal vanity
The brahmacharin should wear
A mala of rudraksha[4] beads
And avoid luxury.

24 The brahmacharin must desist
From all personal grooming
And always remain silent
While bathing, eating, excreting,
Attending to rituals
Or repeating the mantra.

25 The brahmacharin should observe
The strictest vow of celibacy.
If that vow is broken,
Even in a dream,
The brahmacharin should bathe,
Practice pranayama to regain control of the prana,
And become immersed
In repeating the Gayatri mantra.

26 After such purification and with a fixed mind,
The brahmacharin should offer worship
At sunrise and sunset
To the fire, the sun, the guru,
The elders, the cows and the gods.
Then the personal mantra
Should be repeated silently.

27 The brahmacharin should know
That the guru is the Supreme Self ~
To be looked upon not
As a mortal,
But as a representative
And embodiment of all the gods.

28 In the morning and in the evening
It is the duty of the brahmacharin
To bring to the guru
The food and other items

That have been donated
And to eat only what the guru gives.

²⁹ The attitude of the brahmacharin
At all times
Must be to serve the guru with humility:
When the guru takes a walk,
The brahmacharin should walk behind.
When the guru takes a seat,
The brahmacharin should sit close by
With palms together.

³⁰ Adopting these practices
The brahmacharin should remain
In the house of the guru
Until all the scriptural studies
Have been completed.

³¹ The brahmacharin who wishes
To completely know the Self
And the sacred Vedas
Should remain with the guru,
And continuing with all the observances
That befit a brahmacharin,
Should surrender to the guru.

³² Empowered by study
And abandoning all concepts of duality,
The brahmacharin should worship the Self ~
In the guru,
In the ritual fire
And in all of creation.

³³ Those who have chosen
The life of brahmacharya or sannyasa
Should avoid all sexual contact
And sexually suggestive activities.

³⁴ Maintaining purity and cleanliness
By bathing before prayers
At sunrise, noon and sunset;
Sipping water before religious rites;

Worshiping the supreme Self;
Making holy pilgrimages;
Chanting the names of the Supreme;
Avoiding what is not to be touched or eaten;
Controlling speech;
Keeping in mind at all times
The supreme Self of all ~

35 Dear Uddhava, these are the rules
That one who has chosen the life
Of either sannyasa or brahmacharya
Must live by.

36 Thus it is that the brahmacharin
Who lives such a life
Of simplicity, purity and celibacy
Becomes like a blazing fire,
Burning to ashes all past desires
And tendencies.
Free from desire
The brahmacharin will know the Self.

37 However, if after having completed
Scriptural studies in the home of the guru,
The brahmacharin who wishes to return to the family
Should make the appropriate offering to the guru,
Bathe and dress suitably.
Then, taking leave of the guru
At an appointed time,
The brahmacharin may go.

38 Thus the initiate who has been twice-born
May re-enter family life;
May become an anchorite
Living in the forest;
May renounce the world
And become a sannyasin.
Proceeding in this way
From one order of life to the next ~
But never in reverse ~
Is the true path of the varnashrama system.

Whatever the life that is chosen,
The initiated twice-born
Should always remember the Self.

39 If on leaving the guru's hermitage
A householder's life is desired,
Then the twice-born should seek
A partner of good character
And appropriate age,
Who has similar characteristics.
If one is chosen who has different characteristics
And is therefore of a different caste,
The rules for such a marriage
Should be upheld.

40 Performance of ritual offerings
Study of the scriptures
And bestowing charity
Are the duties of all the twice-born.
Teaching of the scriptures,
Officiating at rituals
And the acceptance of gifts
For this service
Are the duties of the brahmin.

41 A brahmin who looks upon
The acceptance of gifts
For officiating at the sacrificial rites
As destructive to austerity,
Independence and reputation
Should take only that grain
Which the farmer has let fall to the ground.

42 The body of a brahmin
Is meant not for passing pleasures
But for austerities and
A continuing pursuit of truth
Which will lead to ultimate Bliss.

43 The brahmin who lives at home
And eats only those foods

Which have been discarded
By the farmer and shopkeeper,
And whose mind is ever fixed
On the supreme Self,
Attains that ultimate liberation.

44 Just as a boat on the ocean
Rescues those that are drowning,
I will uplift from the ocean of suffering
Anyone who rescues a brahmin
Or a devotee from harm.

45 Just as the chief elephant
Vigorously defends itself and the herd,
So the kshatriya king must protect and defend
Himself and all his subjects.

46 A king such as this
Will remove from the kingdom
All that is inauspicious,
And on death this king will ascend
To Indra, king of the gods,
In a chariot as brilliant as the sun.

47 A brahmin who falls on hard times
And becomes incapable of being supported
By the traditional means
May take up the life of a vaishya
Or a kshatriya,
But should never take employment
That would cause
The loss of independence.

48 A kshatriya in adversity
May take up the occupations of a vaishya
Or become a hunter
Or a teacher,
But should never take employment
That would cause the loss of independence.

49 A vaishya in dire straits
May take up the life of a shudra

Or that of an artisan or craftsman.
When the bad times are over
Each person should again adopt
The lifestyle that is in accord
With their own characteristics.

50 One who has chosen the householder's
Life known as grihastha
Should daily study the sacred texts
And offer to the ancestors the mantra Svadha
And to the demigods the mantra Svaha.
Daily worship of all beings should be made
By offering them food and water.
The householder must also always remember
The Self that abides in all beings ~
From the rishis to ordinary people and beasts.
These five practices are the duties
Of this stage of life.

51 People in the grihastha stage of life
Should maintain their dependents
With money that has come through good fortune
Or honest labor.
According to their means
They should host religious ceremonies and rites.

52 No householder should get so attached to family
That the Self is forgotten
Or relegated to second place.
The wise householder will always remember
To hold fast to that which is imperishable
And to let go of that which is perishable.

53 Remember always the associations made
With relatives, spouse, children and friends
Are like the chance meetings of travellers ~
Brief, and only for the duration of this lifetime.
At the end of each life these relationships end ~
Just as a dream ends upon awakening.

54 Keeping such an awareness
The householder can live free from entrapment
In the ideas-of-"I" and -"mine" ~
Even while performing the required duties.

55 A devotee who has thus
Worshiped the Self through householder duties,
May in the fullness of time
And when all duties have been discharged
Retire to the forest to live a hermit's life.
Or, if children have been produced,
The householder may leave it all
And enter the life of a sannyasin.

56 But the householder who gets attached
To property, children and wealth,
Who lives by the dictates of their spouse
And is confused about their true identity,
Is easily bound to ideas-of-"I" and -"mine."

57 Such a person will always be given
To creating reasons for forgetting the Self
And not moving on to the next stage of life.
"Oh," they will say, "My parents are still alive,
My partner cannot cope,
My children cannot live without me."

58 With an unfocused mind
Such a person will continually be distracted
By foolish thoughts of "I" and "mine,"
And on death will go to great darkness.

❋ *Dialogue 13*

My guru, Swami Venkatesananda, always exhorted people not to become pigeon-holed and to use systems only in so far as they allow us to do the best we can. Krishna is emphasizing that, ultimately, whatever the system employed, we are not the people we think we are ~ but the eternal, immortal Self.

In Dialogue 13, Krishna elaborates on the last two stages of life, those of the anchorite and the renunciate. Today we have come to recognize only one stage of life ~ youth and its passions. In contrast, the varnashrama system recognizes that, while we have certain abilities in youth, when we move to adulthood other possibilities present themselves. When the children have matured and our mission in the world has been accomplished, entirely new opportunities open up.

Once our children are independent (usually much earlier than most of us who are parents care to admit), we face a future that looks not towards the beginning of a life but towards its end. We must become courageous and accept the truth: the end that is death is much nearer. Such courage allows us to examine life and death more closely. Until now we have stood on the safe shore of life, casting out the occasional net to discover what is beyond it. But now we take to the sea ~ we sail with death and in so doing discover the eternal life beyond this never-ending cycle of birth, death and rebirth. We do not put out to sea alone. Krishna, through this teaching, is the taraka, the boatman who comes from the opposite shore to guide us across.

1 The Radiant One, Krishna, continued,

When one has completed the duties of grihastha
And wishes to retire from them,
One may leave one's spouse
In the care of the children of the marriage ~
Or one may take the spouse along
And retire to the forest
To devote oneself
To the third stage of the lifespan,
The stage called vanaprashtha.

2 Once retired to the forest,
One should live on only the purest foods ~
Like wild bulbs, roots and fruit.
One should clothe oneself
Only in bark, simple cloth or animal skin,
And sleep on a bed of straw or grass.

3 There one should give up all vanity
And allow the hair on one's head and body to grow.
The body should be plunged in water thrice daily
Without the need for social cleanliness.

4 There the anchorite should sit
In the midst of the five fires in the heat of summer,[1]
And in the lashing rain,
Or immersed in icy water in the cold of winter.
These are the austerities that will be required.

5 The anchorite should eat food
Cooked over a flame or ripened naturally.
Hard foods may be ground with a pestle and mortar
Or against stone ~ or even with the teeth.

6 Having become aware of the place and time
Of the growth of things,
And also of personal digestive powers,
The anchorite should gather food
Only when it is needed ~
And not eat what has been stored.

7 All the seasonal sacrificial rites
Should be performed at the appropriate time
Using wild grains.
Never should the forest anchorite
Use an animal in sacrifice,
Even when enjoined to do so by the Vedas.

8 The Vedas command the anchorite
To perform all those rituals,
Including Agnihotra,[2]
That are performed by the householder.
Thus the rituals of the new moon and the full moon,

And also the rituals of the three four-month seasons
Should all be done.

9 With the body emaciated
By these austerities
The anchorite will reach
The higher realm of the rishis,
And from there
Will be directed to the supreme Self.

10 Uddhava, there is no bigger fool
Than one who engages in all these austerities
Only to gain the fulfillment of passing ambitions.

11 When the anchorite reaches an age
Where due to infirmity
These austerities can no longer be practiced,
The anchorite should place
The sacrificial fire in the center of the heart
And mentally enter the fire.3

12 The anchorite who
Has developed a distaste
For the higher heavenly realms,
Which can be gained only through effort,
May enter the sannyasa4 stage of life.

13 Then, free from all desires,
The sacred rites pertaining to such an occasion
Should be performed,
And all that is still possessed
Should be given away
To enter the fire that is sannyasa.

14 The gods, believing that they
Will be transcended in excellence
By one making such a renunciation,
Will send obstructions through
Spouse and family.

15 If the sannyasin would have a cloth
To cover the body at all

It should only cover the loins.
No personal possessions should be retained
Other than a staff and a pot for drinking water.

16 The sannyasin must take care in walking
Not to step on another creature,
And water to be drunk
Should be strained through a cloth.
A sannyasin must speak
Only those words that ring with truth,
And always act according to conscience.

17 Sannyasins must control their vitality,
And avoid idle talk and action for gain.
One who cannot do this
Is no more a sannyasin
Than the staff that is carried.

18 A sannyasin should beg for food
From households of any of the four castes.
Avoiding the houses of those with reprehensible habits,
The sannyasin must approach
No more than seven houses in all,
And must be satisfied
With whatever is obtained from them.

19 Then going out to the village watering place,
The sannyasin should wash the food gathered
And offer portions to the gods
And to others in need.
Only then may the sannyasin
In silence eat what remains.
Nothing should be saved
Or set aside for another time.

20 Sannyasins should roam the earth
Free of attachments
And with the senses under control.
With a steady mind
And impartial vision
Their only pleasures and pastimes
Should be in seeking the Self.

²¹ Sannyasins should dwell
In a secure but solitary place
With their minds fixed
On the discovery of that Self
That is the same Self in me.

²² Thus the sannyasin should be engaged
In enquiry into the truth
Regarding the nature of bondage
And liberation of the Self.
The sannyasin must discover
The bondage of the senses
And the liberation in their control.

²³ Completely controlling the five senses
And that sixth sense, the mind,
The sage should live a life
Totally detached from trifling pleasures
And immersed in the eternal bliss
Of the Self that is the Self in me.

²⁴ Going to towns, villages, settlements
And places of pilgrimage
Only to beg for food,
The sannyasin should travel the earth
Visiting its sacred places,
Its flowing rivers and soaring mountains
With their deeply penetrating solitude.

²⁵ The sannyasin can also beg for food
At the hermitage of anchorites.
This will be the most pure food
Consisting of grains gathered from the field.
Such food will quickly cleanse
And steady the mind.

²⁶ The sannyasin should not regard
This phenomenal world as real.
With a mind unattached to this world
Or to the next,

The sannyasin should refrain from all activities
Intended to secure worldly pleasure.

27 Through sound reasoning
The sannyasin should come upon the truth
That the body, mind and vitality ~
Regarded so jealously as "I" and "mine" ~
Are nothing but impositions on the Self.
Knowing this, the sannyasin
Should think no more of them
And become established in the Self alone.

28 One for whom
This phenomenal world has grown pale,
Who is steadfastly devoted to me
And wants nothing but the Self,
Should take to the sannyasa life
Regardless of previous station or status
And rise above these petty distinctions.

29 Then, though possessing a sound mind,
The sannyasin should be as spontaneous as a child;
Though intelligent
Behave like a fool;
Though articulate
Speak in riddles;
Though learned in the scriptures
Live like one uncultured.

30 The sannyasin should not expound
The rituals of the Vedas
Nor speak against them.
The sannyasin should not tend
To cynicism or controversy
Nor indulge in vain arguments
Concerning the scriptures.

31 The sannyasin should not provoke
Nor be provoked.
The sannyasin should endure abuse
And never abuse or insult anyone.

For the sake of the perishable body
The sannyasin should create no enmity
For this would be no better
Than one animal preying on another.

³² For just as the one moon is
Reflected in the many receptacles
That hold water,
So is the one supreme Self
That dwells in one's own body
The same Self that dwells in all bodies.

³³ With a balanced mind
The sannyasin should not be overjoyed
To get a little food,
Nor be despondent
When there is none to be had.
The sannyasin should remain content
Knowing that these things depend on destiny.

³⁴ But do not take this to mean
That the sannyasin should make no effort
To procure food.
Such food must be sought
As is necessary to continue living ~
Through which the truth can be reflected on
And the sannyasin can become free.

³⁵ The sage will accept
Whatever food is offered ~
Be it good or bad.
Likewise, the sage will accept
The clothes and bed
That are provided.

³⁶ A sage will observe
All the rules of cleanliness ~
Not because of scriptural injunctions
But because it is the way of the Self.

³⁷ Such a sage
Will have no perception of opposites.

If some such perception still remains
Through the power of personal destiny,
It will disappear on death
When the sage will be united with me.

38 One who is detached from gain in this world
And sees its attendant sorrows,
But who has not received instructions
In attaining the final liberation,
Should go to the dwelling of a guru
To receive the teaching.

39 Such a person should remain there
Serving the guru
With love and faith
As if the guru were the Self,
Until the truth is realized.

40 But one who has not controlled
The senses and the mind,
Who is still attached to the phenomenal world,
Who has not extinguished the desires burning in the heart
But who becomes a sannyasin
In order to make a living ~

41 Such a one
Who denies the body,
Fails to make sacrifices to the gods
And denies the Self ~
Such a one will live a life of desperation
In this world and in the next.

42 The first duties of the sannyasin
Are non-violence and equanimity.
The first duties of the vanaprastha
Are austerity and philosophical understanding.
The first duties of the grihastha
Are sustenance of all living creatures
And the performance of sacrificial rites.
The first duty of the brahmacharin
Is service to the guru.

⁴³ The householder should also practice
Celibacy except at the appropriate time,
Steadfastness in the performance of duties,
Purity of body and mind,
Contentment with life
And friendship towards all living things.
Worship of the Self should be practiced by all.

⁴⁴ Whatever one's duties,
One who worships the Self alone
And is constant in that worship ~
Knowing that the Self is the Self of all beings ~
Will know me as the Self.

⁴⁵ O Uddhava, I am Brahma,
The creator of this universe,
And I am its dissolution.
I am the supreme Self
Beyond creation and dissolution.
Come to me through loving service.

⁴⁶ Thus, by performing your duties
According to your tendencies,
And studying the scriptures,
You will become purified
And you will understand
The supremacy of the Self.

⁴⁷ These duties of the varnashrama system
Steadfastly attended to,
With constant devotion to the Self,
Will lead to perfection
And the Supreme.

⁴⁸ So, my dear and saintly Uddhava,
I have answered your question
And given the means
Whereby everyone,
Attending to their own duty,
May attain the Self.

❀ Dialogue 14

Krishna begins this dialogue by pointing to the value of direct experience, as opposed to mere learning. He goes on to detail the practices that lead to such experience. Practice and experience are the cornerstone of Yoga.

The Yogi is not the kind of philosopher who gives time only to theorizing. The Yogi is required to practice and to have personal experience based on that practice. From this point of view, Yoga is the most difficult path to choose, for the subject of the enquiry is not only the body-mind and its relationship with the perceived world, but also the transcendency beyond body-mind and world. It is this that makes Yoga a science. Any scientist has to prove theories in the practical setting of the laboratory; anyone wishing to duplicate these experiments has to employ exactly the same protocols. In the same way, Yogis have for centuries engaged in scientific practices based on the theory that we are more than we immediately perceive ~ and have arrived at direct experience (pratyaksha) of the ultimate Reality.

In this dialogue, Krishna describes the cosmology of the *Bhagavatham*, vividly portraying how the world of multiplicities came to be perceived. But he keeps pointing us back to the practices that will lead to the experience of Oneness. He also indicates the points of reference to use in this process. Foremost among these are the Vedic scriptures, which record the understanding of those who have experienced ultimate Reality. Then there is our own experience. No matter how caught up we are in the world of phenomena, it is those fleeting but haunting experiences we all have that move us to continue on the spiritual path. Another point of reference is tradition, built into our communities to remind us of our inherently Divine nature. Finally there is inference, the idea of there being no smoke without fire. Given the world of phenomena, a source can be inferred.

These points of reference lead to certain practices, some of which are part of the yama and niyama that readers may have previously encountered in the famous *Patanjali Yoga Sutras*.[1] Krishna enumerates twelve yama and twelve niyama, while Patanjali speaks of five in each category.

[1] The Radiant One, Krishna, continued,

The sannyasin who has learned
All that is required
To know the Self,
And for whom such knowledge
Is not mere theory but direct experience,
And who knows this phenomenal world
To be an illusion,
Such a one,
Known as a vidvat-sannyasin,
Should surrender all that knowledge
And all that experience
To me, the Eternal.

[2] For I am the goal
And the means,
The prosperity and the freedom
From all sorrows
For the Jnana Yogi.
Nothing further beyond me
Need concern the vidvat-sannyasin.

[3] Only those who have been purified
Through both knowledge and experience
Know my true and supreme nature.
Truly, it is these souls that are my support
And are much loved by me.

[4] Austerities, pilgrimages to holy places,
Repetition of prayers and mantras,
And generous acts of charity,
Amount to nothing
Compared to that knowledge
Gained from the experience of Self-realization.

[5] O Uddhava, know yourself
To be ready for this experience.
Once it is gained
Surrender it ~ and its knowledge ~ to me
And continue to worship me with devotion.

6 Having worshiped me
In their own hearts,
And made sacrifice to me
As the inner Being,
Giver of all blessings,
Sages have come to me
And attained the Absolute.

7 My dear Uddhava, the body
Belongs only to the present moment.
It alone is subject
To the three gunas
And the five stages of life ~
Birth, growth, existence,
Transformation and death.
As it is subject to these things
Detach your mind from it:
Identify with the birthless
And deathless Self of all beings
That belongs to eternity.

8 The devotee Uddhava responded,

Beloved, you who are this universe
And that which transcends this universe,
Please tell me
About the pure and ancient teaching,
Which together with dispassion
And transcendent experience,
Leads to you.
Tell me also of the path of devotion
That even the great ones seek to know.

9 For anyone tormented by the pain
Brought through the agencies of fate,
Illness and natural phenomena,
I see your beloved feet as the only shelter ~
Protecting us even while bestowing great blessings.

10 O Great One, lift me up ~
For I have fallen into the pit
Of unremitting pain:

Thirsting for passing pleasures
I lie helpless,
Bitten by the snake of time.
Pour into me that wisdom
By which I may be released.

11 The Radiant One, Krishna, replied,

This question was asked before
By King Yudhishthira
After the great battle of Kurukshetra.
Bhishma, foremost among the righteous,
Answered even as he lay dying,
While everyone assembled to listen.

12 After that bloody battle had ended
Yuddhisthira, descendant of Bharata,
Was overwhelmed by the destruction.
Having heard many religious principles,
He entreated Bhishma to give him
That certain teaching
By which liberation may be attained.

13 That teaching ~ rich with knowledge,
Dispassion, faith, devotion and realization ~
I commend to you
Just as Bhishma taught it.

14 I confirm that knowledge according to which
The knower knows
That all of these parts ~
The nine:
~ Prakriti, the creative principle;
~ Purusha, the Self;
~ Mahat Tattva, the field of intelligence;
~ Ahamkara, the idea-of-"I";
~ Tanmatras, the five subtle elements of matter:
   Sound, touch, form, taste and smell;
The eleven:
~ Jnanendriyas, the five organs of perception:
   Nose, tongue, eye, skin and ear;
~ Karmendriyas, the five organs of action:

Reproductive, excretive, feet, hands and ears;
~ Manas, the mind;
The five:
~ Prithvi, earth;
~ Apas, water;
~ Agni, fire;
~ Vayu, air;
~ Akasha, space;
And the three gunas:
~ Sattva, balance;
~ Rajas, activity;
~ Tamas, inertia ~
Permeate all of creation,
From Brahma to the smallest amoeba,
And that the one Supreme
Pervades them all.

¹⁵ This knowledge becomes a realization
When one no longer sees multiplicities
Pervaded by the One,
But experiences the One as the only reality.
That experience alone,
When life permeated by the gunas
Is seen as a play
Of coming into being,
Continuing and then dissolving,
Is the ultimate knowledge known as vijnana.

¹⁶ That alone should be experienced as real,
Which existed before the beginning,
Which is present during the existence
And which will continue to be after the end.
That which accompanies this evolution of being
And yet survives it ~
That alone should be experienced as real.

¹⁷ Of the many means of perception
Which can corroborate this knowledge
These four are the most authoritative:
Those Vedas which teach it,

Direct experience of the transcendent Reality,
Tradition which upholds its truth
And inference which points to a phenomenal world
That cannot exist without a cause.
In none of these can an experience
Of multiplicities find support.
Understanding this
The wise turn
From the experience of the many
Towards experience of the One.

18 The wise must understand
That the rewards of heaven
Promised by religious rituals,
Are as transient
As pleasures on earth.

19 O Uddhava ~ you who are without blemish,
Understand that the religious practice
Most conducive to success
Is devotion to the Self.
Let me explain again
The practice of such devotion.

20 Develop faith
By listening constantly
To stories of me.
Sing songs of praise
And become attached to me alone.
Let all your prayers
Be directed to me.

21 Worship me
With your body:
In worshipful devotion
Prostrate before me,
Who abides in all beings
And in my devotees.

22 Surrender your mind to me:
Do this by surrendering
All your actions to me.

Speak of me only
And my transcendent nature
And all desires will be banished.

23 Forsake riches, pleasures and even happiness
For my sake.
Do good deeds and give in charity
For my sake.
Do the fire ceremony
Chanting my name.
Practice austerities and make vows,
All for my sake.

24 Dear friend, those who have
Undertaken such practices,
Who have surrendered themselves
In loving devotion to me,
Are filled by me.
There are no other religious practices
That remain to be done by them.

25 When the consciousness
Is fixed on the Self
It becomes peaceful and sattvic.
Then one's religion is strengthened,
And one comes to knowledge,
Proper detachment and true power.

26 But when the awareness
Is fixed on fleeting
Things of the senses,
Which are pursued
Through the organs of action,
The mind becomes rajasic
And these four qualities evaporate.

27 That which engenders devotion
Is the best religious practice.
That which enables
The experience of the One
Behind the multiplicity,
Is the best knowledge.

The best detachment is disinterest
In the objects of the world.
And from all of these
Flows true splendor.

28 The devotee Uddhava asked,

O Radiant One, Krishna,
Enemy of the enemies of the Self,
What are the yamas
And how many are there?
And what are the niyamas?
What constitutes self-control,
And how will I know
When I have achieved balance?
What is tolerance
And what is steadiness?
Tell me please, Beloved.

29 What is charity?
What is austerity?
What is courage?
What is honesty?
What is renunciation?
What is wealth worth coveting?
What is religious sacrifice,
And what is the proper remuneration
To the teacher or the priest?

30 Most Beloved, tell me,
What is the real strength of a person?
What is real profit and gain?
What is real knowledge
And what is real humility?
What is beauty
And what are joy and sorrow?

31 Who is the true sage
And who is the fool?
Which is the correct path
And which is the false one?
What is heaven

And what is hell?
Who is truly a friend
And what may be called home?

32 Who is rich
And who is poor?
Who is the taker
And who is the giver?
O Ruler of the Virtuous,
Please answer these questions.

33 The Radiant One, Krishna, replied,

Non-violence,
Truthfulness,
Refraining from coveting,
Non-attachment,
Humility,
Never seeking to possess anything,
Respect for religious principles,
Living in Brahman,
Silence and steadiness,
Forbearance and courage;

34 Bodily cleanliness and purity of mind,
Repetition of the mantra,
Austerities and faith,
Hospitality and worship,
Pilgrimages to holy places,
Always seeking and acting
For the good of all beings,
Contentment
And service of the guru.

35 These, my dear friend,
Are the twelve yamas and the twelve niyamas.
Practiced faithfully
They grant happiness and fulfillment.

36 The mind becomes calm
Only when fixed on the Self.
The most perfect self-control

Is control of the senses.
Tolerance is the bearing of sorrow,
And steadiness is control of the senses,
The tongue and the sexual impulse.

37 The greatest charity
Is to relinquish any thought
Of violence towards others.
Austerity is the renunciation
Of all hopes and desires.
Courage is overcoming
One's own tendencies.
Honesty is looking upon all
With impartial vision.

38 Truthfulness is speech that is kind
And which even the sages may praise.
Purity is non-attachment
To the results of one's actions,
While renunciation is the acceptance
Of the sannyasa stage of life.

39 A spiritual life is the wealth
That should be coveted.
I, the supreme Self,
Am the religious sacrifice.
The teaching of knowledge
Is the ultimate religious remuneration,
And control of the vitality
Is true strength.

40 True fortune and splendor
Are my own divine Self.
Profit and gain
Are devotion to me.
Real knowledge
Is the knowledge which ends
All multiplicities.
Real humility
Is avoiding wrongful actions.

41 True beauty is desirelessness.
Happiness is equanimity
In both joy and sorrow.
Sorrow is the ceaseless longing
For gratification of the senses.
A true sage
Is one who can distinguish
Between bondage and liberation.

42 A fool is one who has identified
With only the body and personality.
The right path is that
Which leads to me.
The wrong path is the one
That causes confusion.
Heaven is the sattvic mind.

43 Hell is the tamasic mind.
The teacher in whom I abide
Is the only true friend.
O Uddhava, the human body
May be called home.
One who is virtuous
May be called wealthy.

44 A poor person
Is one who is never satisfied.
A wretched person
Is one who has never conquered the senses.
Only those who are detached from
The objects of the senses
Are masters of themselves.

45 Now I have answered your questions, Uddhava,
And there is nothing to be gained
From continuing the discussion in this direction.
What are the definitions of good and evil?
Judging another to be good or bad is evil.
To cease making judgments between good and bad,
That is true goodness.

This is a dialogue of practical instruction invaluable to anyone on the path of Yoga. Uddhava asks for clarification of the statement Krishna made at the end of the last dialogue. He points out that the Vedas weigh heavily towards the very judgments about good and evil that Krishna exhorts us not to make. There is no simple answer to Uddhava's question, and Krishna does not dismiss it with an attempt at simplicity. Instead, he describes the three paths to spiritual enlightenment ~ Karma Yoga (the path of action), Jnana Yoga (the path of knowledge) and Bhakti Yoga (the path of devotion). We choose the spiritual path that suits our current tendencies and position. As in our relations with the world, we act out who we are. However, injunctions concerning good and bad actions that are applicable in the world cease to have any meaning on a spiritual journey.

If we have grown tired of the world, even of religious actions that promise a reward in this world or the next, we will be drawn to the path of intellectual understanding. If we feel that there is still work to be done, we will be drawn to the path of action. For those who are in neither or even both of these categories, the path of devotion and faith will be the way. Each path requires certain practices but these are beyond the boundaries of "good" or "bad" ~ because the spiritual traveller is no longer concerned with "getting results" from actions. Krishna also points out that not to be walking one of these paths is to be wandering endlessly through the cycle of births and deaths.

There is a beautiful teaching in this dialogue regarding the place of the human body in the spiritual journey. It is, Krishna says, the ideal vehicle for crossing the ocean of samsara. The word samsara can be translated as "conditioned existence" ~ the opposite of existence without boundaries. The human body alone is the vehicle of enlightenment because we need it to engage in the practices required of our chosen path.

[1] The devotee Uddhava said,

O Lotus-eyed One,
You truly are

An embodiment of the Vedas,
So tell me,
Do they not give clear instructions
In both prescribed and prohibited actions?

2 Do not the Vedas
Speak of a distinction
Even in the varnashrama system
Between good and bad actions?
For example, the merits and demerits
Of those born in mixed-caste marriages.
And do not these same Vedas
Speak of heaven and hell
Based on good and bad actions
Committed in a lifetime?

3 How can we reconcile your words ~
That in order to attain liberation
We should cease making judgments
About good and bad actions ~
With the injunctions of the Vedas?

4 Beloved One, your word
Is surely the highest Veda,
Which offers light
To the ancestors, the gods
And humans alike,
Conferring grace on all
And knowledge of both
The seen and the unseen
Purpose of life.

5 The distinction between good and evil
Can come only through your instruction,
Which is the Vedas,
And not from our own intuition.
However, your command
To cease to make such judgments
Has created some confusion for me.
Please enlighten me.

6 The Radiant One, Krishna, spoke,

There are three paths
To spiritual enlightenment:
The Yoga of knowledge, jnana;
The Yoga of action, karma;
The Yoga of devotion, bhakti.
Other than these three
There is no other way.

7 The path of Jnana Yoga is for those
Who have lost all interest
In the rewards promised by action.
The path of Karma Yoga is for those
Who still have an interest
In the workings of the world
And the happiness of all people.

8 For those who have been infused
With an intense devotion of the Self,
Who delight in knowledge of the Self
And in tales and songs of the Self,
Who are neither disinterested in the world
Nor attached to it,
For such people
There is the path of Bhakti Yoga.

9 You should engage in your duties
Until you lose interest in the world,
Or until an intense faith and devotion
Arise in your heart.

10 Uddhava, any person
Properly discharging their own duties
Without desire for a reward
Will go neither to heaven nor hell
As long as they avoid evil.

11 Such a person,
Even while living
And working in the world,

Will either reach pure knowledge
Or develop a deep faith and devotion.

12 Those who dwell in hell
And likewise
Those who dwell in heaven
Covet a life in this world
Because this world offers the opportunity
For both knowledge and devotion.
Neither heaven nor hell
Hold this promise.

13 A wise person
Prizes neither heaven nor hell ~
Nor even to return again
To this world,
Where attachment to "I" and "mine"
Is an enchantment
In which one can get lost.

14 Conscious of this, the wise
Diligently strive for liberation
Here and now
Before death comes.
For this body, though mortal,
Is the means
By which liberation is attained.

15 A bird, seeing the tree
In which it built its nest
Being cut down,
Abandons it,
O Uddhava.

16 One trembles with fear
At the realization
That the days and nights of one's life
Are being cut down.
The wise seeing this
Give up attachment to the body ~
Just as the bird

Relinquishes attachment for its nest,
And gains peace.

17 This blessed human form,
Which is so difficult to obtain
Although in easy reach,
Is like a sturdy boat
With the guru at its helm
And me the wind in its sails,
On which one may cross
This ocean of samsara.
Anyone who does not see this
And does not strive to make the crossing,
Seeks to negate the Self.

18 The Yogi who is disinterested
In the results of actions,
Having realized the true nature
Of this world and its rewards,
Turns to the Self:
Taking control of the mind
Through all the prescribed practices,
The Yogi fixes it on the distant shore of the Self.

19 Once committed to this course,
If the mind should wander
The Yogi with full consciousness
Uses the prescribed methods
For regaining control.

20 Once the mind is under control,
By mastering the vitality
And the senses,
The Yogi, with an awareness
Charged by sattva guna,
Remains ever watchful.

21 This process of controlling the mind
Can be likened to
Taming a wild horse:
Little by little

Learning when to slacken the reins
And when to draw them in.
This practice is the first step
Towards the highest Yoga.

²² Allow the mind to contemplate
The nature of material creation
And its evolution
Towards inevitable and final dissolution.
Let the mind work forwards
And backwards through this
Until it becomes calm.

²³ In this manner,
The mind will lose interest
In the temporary phenomena of this world
And will cease to identify with them.
Then it will develop dispassion
And come to ponder
The teachings of the guru.

²⁴ The mind should be kept
Constantly engaged in
Contemplating the Self,
Enquiring into the nature of the Self,
And worshiping the Self
While holding to
The disciplines of the yama and the niyama.
No other way forward is possible.

²⁵ The Yogi who commits a contemptible act
Through a momentary lapse of attention
Must burn the results of that act
Through the discipline of Yoga alone,
And not resort to petty penances.

²⁶ Adherence to the duties that accord with
One's tendencies and stage of life
Is prescribed as meritorious.
But the prohibition of certain actions
And the prescribing of others

Was set in place
Only to create detachment
From all actions
Once their limited nature was realized.

²⁷ For one who has become
Devoted to the Self
But is unable to renounce
The pleasures of this world

²⁸ I prescribe joyful
And continuing devotion
To the Self
Even while enjoying   *
The pleasures of the world.
But the ephemeral nature of these pleasures
Should always be remembered.

²⁹ For such a person,
Constantly worshiping me
Through this path of devotion,
All desires of the heart will be destroyed ~
For I, the Self, dwell in the heart.

³⁰ When the Yogi then sees the Self,
The terrible knot that binds the heart ~
The idea-of-"I" ~
Will be cut asunder:
All doubts will be resolved,
All karma exhausted,
And I, the Self of the universe,
Will be realized.

³¹ Thus for the Yogi
Who has chosen the path of bhakti
Neither knowledge nor dispassion
Is conducive to grace.

³² That which is acquired through action,
That which is acquired through austerities,
That which is acquired through knowledge,
That which is acquired through dispassion,

That which is acquired through Yoga disciplines,
That which is acquired through charitable acts,
That which is acquired through auspiciousness,
Indeed that which is acquired
Through any other means that one can think of,

33 Is also acquired
Through this path of devotion,
Which grants freedom from misery,
Liberation
And even a sojourn in heaven
If it is desired.

34 Those who are devoted to the Self
Seek nothing else ~
Not even freedom
From the cycle of birth and death.

35 The greatest contentment
Comes from devotion alone
And not from its rewards,
Therefore one who has this devotion
Seeks nothing else.

36 Merits and demerits
Acquired through virtue or vice
Do not attach themselves
To one who has attained
Even-minded devotion
And realized the Self,
Which lies beyond the veil of the mind.

37 Those who follow
Any one of these three paths
That I have just shown you
Will reach the Self
That is at the beating heart of all things
And which transcends all things.

This is the dialogue for anyone who yearns for a direct experience of the Divine. In the *Bhagavatham*, Krishna is a challenger of the status quo, opposing the Vedic emphasis on ritual. When Nanda, his foster father, insists on ritual to propitiate Indra for rain, Krishna scoffs:

> *Hah! Clouds and rain are natural phenomena. Natural laws conduct them. If there is a god such as Indra at all, he too must know these laws and know also that they have absolutely nothing to do with him.*
> (Book 10, 14: 8–23)

As Krishna unceremoniously takes the power of the spiritual path out of the hands of priests and clergy and gives it to the seeker, he can only remind us of another great avatar. Like Christ, Krishna dismisses those who purport to have exclusive control of knowledge. It is not through correctness of ritual that we will achieve salvation but through the power of our own understanding.

Krishna again refers to the tattvas, here earth, water, fire, air and space. Tattva is often translated as "element," which loses some of the meaning. The literal translation is "thatness." Everything is made from these five "thatnesses," which give us our individual characteristics. We are accustomed to thinking of ourselves as sophisticated machines with moving parts that can break down (and even be replaced). Here is a completely different vision. We are reflected in nature ~ in its rich earth, its flowing waters, its raging fires, its rushing winds. The five tattvas are woven into all of us but the predominance of a particular tattva will distinguish one person from another. Look at wind, for example: it arrives, changes everything and then moves on. This is a perfect description of someone with leadership abilities, who can move others and get the job done ~ in other words, a kshatriya. Or space, which separates one thing from another, in which chaos becomes order. Space gives us the ability to separate the real from the unreal, the truth from fiction ~ in short, a brahmin. Thus through these tattvas we are all parts of the same whole, while each individual is made unique by their particular combination in us.

The final verse is probably the most powerful in the entire dialogue. It is one which can form the basis of a lifelong meditation.

¹ The Radiant One, Krishna, said,

Those who choose to walk
Neither the path of knowledge,
Nor the path of action,
Nor the path of faithful devotion,
Will wander through this world
Restlessly seeking satisfaction
Through petty desires
From birth to death to birth again.

² Be devoted to your own path,
And do not try to walk
The path of another:
This is the criterion of purity
If one is a spiritual traveller.

³ O Uddhava,
You who are without stain,
Understand clearly that
Any evaluation of good or evil,
Right or wrong
Must be relevant to the context
In which it is made:
Whether it is a worldly and social activity,
A religious activity
Or done for physical survival.

⁴ These evaluations
Of good and bad,
Pure and impure,
Were originally given by me
To the gods and the ancestors,
As a guide
To how to conduct one's life
Without offending against any religious practices.

⁵ Emanating from the one supreme Self
Came earth, water, fire, air and space ~
These five constitute both the seen
And the unseen of all bodies:
From Brahma through to human beings,

Nature and even solid rock ~
All are pervaded by these five,
And through these five
Each is allocated its own nature.

6 O Uddhava,
Though everyone is made
From these same five
The Vedas have fashioned
Diverse names and duties
Like brahmin, kshatriya and so on,
So that each one
May achieve the purpose
Of his or her own nature.

7 Saintly one,
In order to establish
A division of labor
I have given guidelines
For that which is righteous
And that which is unrighteous,
Pertaining to all things
That are constrained by time and space.

8 Land that is untrodden by deer
Should be considered unholy land.
Land that is trodden by deer
But in which the wise are not heard
And their words are not worshiped
Should be considered unholy land.
Any lands
In which the wise do not dwell
Are truly lands without sanctity.[1]

9 If an object or a particular time
Is suitable or appropriate
For performing one's duty
Then it should be considered pure.
But if the object ceases
To be able to do
What it was made for

Then it is impure.
If the time
Is not an appropriate time
Then it is impure.

10 The purity or impurity of an object
Can also be determined
By things external to the object itself:
For instance, by an authority on the subject;
By undergoing certain processes;
By the passage of time;
And by the degree
And relative purity or impurity
Of these means.

11 Objects that are impure
May or may not impart
Impurity to the user.
This will depend on the
Potency of the impurity,
And on one's own understanding,
Strength, reaction, integrity
And physical condition.

12 The purity of objects such as grains
And liquids such as ghee,[2]
Or objects made of wood,
Ivory, metals, textiles
And even objects made of skins,
Will depend upon time
And their exposure
To the elements.

13 A purification process is appropriate
When it removes dirt,
Odor or contamination
And returns the object
To its original state.

14 All those who have been initiated
Should purify themselves
Before conducting religious duties.

One can be cleansed of impurity
By bathing;
By acts of charity;
Through austerities;
By fulfilling your duties;
By acts of ritual purification;
Or by remembrance of me.

15 The above six
Will lead to purity,
And their opposites to impurity.
The purity of a mantra
Depends on the understanding
One has of it.
The purity of actions
Depends on their being offered
To the supreme Self.

16 According to the Vedas
That which appears to be pure
Can in reality be impure,
While that which appears impure
Can in reality be pure.
Thus these words of the Vedas
Cut off at the root
Categorical judgment of what is pure
And what is impure.

17 Someone already on the ground
Has no further to fall:
Actions that would debase one person
May not have the same effect on another.
These things will depend
On the status of the one performing the action.

18 Whatever one refrains from
One is liberated from.
This is the basis of renunciation
And of a spiritual life
That will lead to freedom
From illusion, fear and suffering.

¹⁹ The value you place on an object
Will determine
The strength of your desire for it,
And the power of your attachment to it.
It is this desire and attachment
That leads people to quarrel.

²⁰ Such quarreling leads to anger,
And anger leads to a darkness
In consciousness.
From then on
The capacity
To know right from wrong
Is clouded.

²¹ O noble Uddhava,
Such people
Whose consciousness is clouded
Are reduced to nought:
They lose their true purpose
And mission in life,
And stumble in a stupor
Towards certain death.

²² Losing oneself
In gratification of the senses
One knows neither one's self
Nor the Self of all.
Then one lives uselessly,
Merely breathing in and out,
Which even a tree
Or a blacksmith's bellows can do.

²³ Those injunctions of the Vedas
That promise a reward for good actions
Are meant to entice people towards good ~
Like promising sweets to a child
Being asked to swallow bitter medicine.

²⁴ This is because human beings
Are inherently attached
To the idea of reward.

25 Think about it, Uddhava:
How else could the Vedas
Persuade people wandering aimlessly
Towards certain death
To do what ought to be done
And move towards enlightenment?

26 Only ignorant people
Who do not understand
The true teaching of the Vedas
Insist on these injunctions
And speak of reward and punishment
For actions done.
Those who know the Vedas
Do not speak of these things.

27 Those who are caught in the darkness
Of passion, greed and miserliness
Are blinded by the light
Of the fire that is the Vedas:
Heedlessly they indulge in ritualistic acts ~
Only to choke on the smoke
Of their own ignorance.

28 A strict adherence to ritual
Will be their only theme:
They will not even recognize me
Dwelling in their own heart
And in the heart of this entire creation.
At the end of their lives,
With their vision clouded by
The fog of ignorance,
They will not see
That which is so close at hand.

29 These people,
Committed as they are
To the world of objects
And its rewards,
And to violence
By means of ritual,

Cannot understand
The words of the Vedas
That I am now imparting.

30 In sacrificial rituals
These cruel people
Will slaughter innocent animals
In order to make offerings
To ancestors, gods and spirits
All for the gratification
Of their own desires.
Such violence has never been
An instruction of the Vedas.

31 They fantasize in their own minds
About a heavenly world
That comes after this one,
And then imagine
That like merchants in a market
They can trade rituals
For a place in such a heaven.)

(32 Bound by rajas, tamas and sattva,
They worship the gods
And Indra, king of the gods,
Who is himself
Tied up by the power of the gunas.
They fail to see me
And they fail to worship me.)

(33 These people fondly imagine
That by engaging in these rituals
They will enjoy a time in heaven
And then return to earth
To be born into a noble and wealthy family.)

34 Alas!
Their pride and greed blinds them
To the real message of the Vedas.)

35 The subject matter of the Vedas
Is these three:

(Conduct, worship and knowledge.
They hold as supreme
That knowledge by which the individual
Realizes his or her true cosmic nature.
But this teaching of the Vedas
Is not direct
And I am pleased by that.

36 The Vedas are the manifestation
Of Brahman through words.
Comprehension of them will depend
On the state of the prana, the mind,
The senses and the awareness.
But always know that these Vedas
Are like the ocean ~
Deep and unfathomable.

37 As the omnipresent, omniscient
And omnipotent Brahman
I have placed the words of the Vedas
In every being
As the eternal sound of Om ~
The sound without sound ~
As imperceptibly subtle as the lotus stalk.3

38 Just as the spider sends its web
From the depths of its heart
Out through its mouth,
So the universal Supreme
Sends the sound of the sacred Om
From the depths of Its heart
To manifest as the vibrations of sound
Which form the vowels
And consonants of the alphabet.4

39 The alphabet then becomes
The words of the Vedas,
Which expand outwards
In thousands of directions.
This expansion ~
Enriched by the entire range

Of the alphabet's sounds ~
Never ceases.

40 The sacred Om
Is fashioned by the vowels
And from it
Flow all other sounds.
All these sounds form the meters
That become the Vedas ~
And then they will be
Withdrawn again
Into the heart of the Supreme.

41 Of these meters
The gayatri has twenty-four letters,
The ushnik has twenty-eight,
The brihati has thirty-two,
The pankti has thirty-six,
The trishtup has forty,
The jagati has forty-four,
The atitcchanda has forty-eight,
The atijagati has fifty-two,
Completing the full range of sound.

42 The true message of the Vedas
Is known only by me ~
Not by those who give instructions
And indulge in rituals.

43 I am the sacrifice that the Vedas speak of.
I am the supreme Reality that is the object of worship.
I am the knowledge of the Vedas
And the refutation of that knowledge.
I am the transcendent sound of the Vedas,
Which manifests as the material world of multiplicities,
And which ultimately leads those who hear it
To an experience of Oneness.

This is one of the most exciting dialogues of the *Uddhava Gita*. It goes directly to the heart of the problem ~ are we distinct from the transcendent Reality, or are we always at one with it? Krishna ended the previous dialogue by stating that the Self is the Whole: all knowledge, all conduct, all multiplicities. Uddhava opens this dialogue by asking why then teach about "parts" of the whole?

Debate about duality and non-duality has found its way into many cultures. René Descartes, the seventeenth-century European philosopher-scientist, articulated the argument well and came down firmly on the side of two ~ duality ~ that is the existence of a soul distinct from the body. However, in Descartes' scheme, mind and soul seem to be the same thing. The soul (mind) comes equipped with the means for rationalization and the principles of logic are its dynamic.

But to the classical Indian philosopher, soul and mind are not interchangeable. Mind is one of the "vehicles" of the Self, one of the ways in which it moves from an unmanifest to a manifest state; but we must never confuse thinking, analyzing and reasoning ~ all functions of the mind ~ with the Self. The mind is part of the world of maya, constantly seeking to measure, to create limitations. One of the most beautiful metaphors explaining this perspective is to be found in the *Katha Upanishad*. The individual is likened to a chariot ~ the horses are the senses, the reins are the mind, the chariot is the body and the charioteer is the conscious awareness; while the road is the field in which the individual operates. Seated in the back of the chariot is the true owner ~ the Self. The charioteer who forgets this eternal Presence will become absorbed in the field of action and the chariot will continue without purpose or direction. It is by remembrance of the Self that control of the chariot is maintained and the goal ~ full realization of the Self ~ is reached.

However, the question of duality still remains. Is that which is embodied and the embodiment one whole or two distinct things? There are three schools of thought on this subject, which weave their way through all Hindu philosophy. Each has commentaries supporting its view on all the great scriptures, including the *Uddhava Gita* and the

Bhagavad Gita. The three schools are the dvaitist (dualist), advaitist (non-dualist) and vishishadvaitist (qualified non-dualist).

Most interpretations of this dialogue seem to indicate that Krishna comes down on the side of dualism, and for a long time I believed that myself. Then reading the dialogue one day I experienced the strong feeling that he was supporting none of these views. We cannot isolate this dialogue but must grasp it in the context of the rest of the text. Earlier, Krishna says:

> *Whatever you see, hear or touch ~*
> *Know that you cannot know it*
> *For what it is.*
> (2:7)

This statement helps us to better understand Krishna when he states that as long as we function through the mind we will have a model of reality rather than Reality itself.

Krishna points out that any experience of "parts" of the Whole will be valid because it is based on a personal understanding of a whole present in any and all of the parts. This is an astonishingly modern idea. The great modern physicist Max Bohm refers to this as "unbroken wholeness." Krishna articulates it in Verse 8 as "In any one part, the other parts are present." And he said this before the invention of electron microscopes and particle accelerators!

If the Whole is present in all the multiplicities, is it distinct from the multiplicities or not? Krishna answers this in the only way possible ~ with a paradox. Yes, the Whole is distinct, he indicates, when viewed through the lens of the multiplicities. No, the multiplicities are not distinct, when viewed through the lens of the Whole. Our ability to see reality, Krishna is saying, depends on the position we take when we look. And the practices we take up are to get us into the right position.

[1] The devotee Uddhava asked,

Please clarify the confusion,
Beloved Teacher of Teachers,
About the parts

That make up the whole of creation.
Just earlier you spoke of the twenty-eight parts
That are divided into nine, eleven, five and three.[1]

2 Yet others speak of twenty-six,
And still others argue
That there can be only twenty-five.
In fact, many numbers are bandied about:
Some speak of seven,
Others say nine or six or four,
Others even eleven or thirteen.

3 All these sages,
Experiencing the Infinite
Through these parts,
Came up with different numbers.
Please clear up this confusion for us.

4 The Radiant One, Krishna, replied,

Whatever these sages have declared,
They all speak the truth, despite their differences.
Because the whole is present in each part
Each personal experience will be different
And still encompass the truth.
The sages who enumerated these parts
Knew well that they were speaking
From under the umbrella of my maya.

5 When you hear people argue,
"No, it is not this number ~ it is that,"
Know that they are arguing
Under the sway of rajas, tamas and sattva ~
So very hard not to succumb to.

6 It is the very disturbance of these gunas
That creates this contention.
All such silly arguments vanish
When evenness of mind
And control of the senses is reached.

7 O best of men,
Depending on the mix

Of tattvas in each person
Each will argue and choose
According to their nature.

8 In any one part
The other parts are present,
Such as space being present in sound.
Gross parts will be present in the subtle,
And the subtle unseen will be present in the gross.

9 Considering that all parts
Are present in the one part,
I simply accept as truth
Whatever number a sage presents
As the result of a personal experience.

10 Some will say that
Because every person is bound by time and space
It is not possible for one to know the Self
That is unbound.
Therefore, they say, there must be
Another transcendent Reality
Which is quite separate from the experiencer,
And which makes possible
An experience of the Unbound.

11 Yet others will say
That there is no difference
Between the individual being
And the unbound, limitless Self,
And that it is the state of sattva
That makes such experience possible.

12 Prakriti they will say,
Made up of the three gunas
Rajas, tamas and sattva,
Alone is responsible for creation,
Sustenance and dissolution,
Not the Self.

13 According to this argument
Knowledge comes from sattva,

Action comes from rajas and
Ignorance comes from tamas;
Time is the agitating agent
Of these three,
And all of them are embodied
In the idea-of-"I."

14 I have enumerated
Nine essential parts:
Purusha and Prakriti,
Manifest creation,
The idea-of-"I,"
Space, air, fire, water and earth.

15 The ears that hear,
The skin that feels,
The eyes that see,
The nose that smells,
And the tongue that tastes ~
These are the five senses
Through which we acquire knowledge.
The voice, the hands, the genitals,
The anus and the feet ~
These are the five organs of action.
The mind is infused
In both these categories.

16 Sound, touch, form, odor and taste,
Are the objects of the five senses
Through which we acquire knowledge.
Speech, action, procreation,
Excretion and movement
Are the functions of the
Five organs of action.

17 At the inception of creation
Prakriti, through the power of the gunas,
Undergoes a transformation
That brings all these parts of creation
Into being.
Purushu gazes upon it.

18 The gaze of Purusha
Empowers the embryonic creation,
Which is sustained by Prakriti.
The constituent parts which are empowered
By the transforming gaze of Purusha
Become the manifest universe.

19 One view is that there are seven constituent parts ~
Namely earth, water, fire, air and space,
Plus the individual self
And the cosmic Self,
Which is the ground
Of both the experiencer
And the object of the experience;
And that from these seven,
The body, the senses and the prana
All emerge.

20 Another view is that there are six
Essential parts to creation,
Namely, the five tattvas
Of earth, water, fire, air and space,
And a sixth part, the supreme Self.
In this view
The supreme Self
Is endowed with these five parts ~
From which it manifests creation
And into which it infuses itself.

21 Others propose the existence
Of just four basic constituents:
Fire, water and earth,
Which all emanate from the Self.
In this view all of creation
Springs from these four.

22 There are others that will number
Seventeen essential parts:
The five tattvas of earth, water, fire, air and space,
The five objects bound to the senses,

The five senses bound to these objects,
Along with the mind and the Self.

23 Those that calculate sixteen basic parts
Differ from the above only in that
The Self and the mind are not distinct.
The five tattvas, the five senses,
The mind, the individual self
And the supreme Self,
Would make thirteen basic parts.

24 If the count is eleven essential parts
Then that is made up of
The Self, earth, water, fire, air and space
And the five senses.
In the count of nine
There is earth, water, fire, air and space,
The mind, the intelligence, the idea-of-"I"
And the supreme Self.

25 So as you can see
The sages have enumerated the parts
In different ways.
Each proposal is presented
With sound reasoning behind it.
Indeed, each one is to be recommended
For the judicious thought that has gone into it.

26 The devotee Uddhava said,

Beloved, although Prakriti, creation,
And Purusha, the supreme Self,
Appear to be distinct,
There also appears to be
No difference between them and
One is never without the other.
Likewise the Self appears to be
Within the body ~
And it is this combination
That is perceived as "I."

27 O Lotus-eyed One,
Please clear up my confusion
In this matter
Through the power of your words.

28 Since it is from you
That all knowledge arises,
And since it is you
That can take it away,
Only you truly know
The extent of your power.

29 The Radiant One, Krishna, said,

This body and the rest of creation
Known as Prakriti,
Is subject to change
Due to the disturbance of the three gunas.
Purusha, the supreme Self,
Is not subject to change.
Therefore there is a difference.

30 My sweet friend,
This manifest world
That can be measured and analyzed,
Consists of the three gunas
And through the gunas
Creates endless multiplicities.
However, these multiplicities
Come under three broad categories:
That Self pervading each object,
The divine agency
By which each object exists and moves,
And the thing itself.

31 The eye,
An object being looked at,
And the light of the sun
Reflecting on the object and the iris of the eye,
All depend on one another
To be revealed.

And yet, even without vision,
Or lighting up an object,
Or reflecting on the eye,
The sun still remains
Distinct and independent.
So it is with the Self.
The Self of all beings
Is the source of all objects
And also the agency
By which all are revealed.
The Self simultaneously remains
Distinct and independent.

32 So understand:
The entire field of consciousness,
The senses, the objects they are bound to,
The organs of action and their actions,
And the subtle agencies which are behind them ~
Namely the individual consciousness,
The mind, the intelligence and the idea-of-"I" ~
The whole of it can be analyzed
Using the three categories I have given you.

33 The continual argument
That revolves around the issue
Of whether or not
The Self is distinct from creation ~
Whether Purusha
Is distinct from Prakriti,
And whether the Self is real or not
Is based on ignorance of the Self;
And it can only apply to a world
Of material dualities and multiplicities.
Those who have turned away from the Self
Are the ones that engage in the argument.

34 The devotee Uddhava asked,

Tell me, O Great Protector,
How do those whose minds
Have been turned away from you

And those who are committed
To action and reward,
Come to be reborn high or low,
Engage in activity for a time
And then give up the body?

35 I seek to know how the Self
That is present everywhere at all times
Passes from one body to another ~
Allotting action to the actionless,
Birth to the birthless
And death to the deathless.
Deluded by your maya
Few can understand this.

36 The Radiant One, Krishna, replied:

The mind, joined with the senses,
The organs of action
Like the hands and the feet,
And the objects that the senses sense,
Becomes set on a course by the actions taken
During the lifetime of a person.
It moves from one world to another
On this course
And the Self is alongside it.

37 The mind thus bound
To the results of those actions,
Remaining fixed on the objects
It experiences through the senses
Or on the Vedas that it hears repeated,
Comes and goes repeatedly.

38 When the mind thus comes and goes
Passing from body to body,
It enters a body and becomes entranced
By the objects surrounding it:
It forgets the past body
And identifies only with the present body.
This forgetfulness of the Self
Is called death.

39 O most generous Uddhava,
What is called birth is no more
Than the identification of the mind
With a new body.
That new body is accepted as reality ~
Just as a body in a dream
Is accepted as reality.

40 Just as the dreamer
Does not remember who he or she was
In a dream gone by,
So the mind
Does not remember
Any previous existence.

41 And just as the dreamer
Conjures up many bodies,
So this threefold division ~
The Self of each being or object,
The agency by which
That being or object exists and moves,
And the being or object itself ~
Conjures up a world of multiplicities
That it enters into relationships with.

42 Dear Uddhava,
Creation is in a constant state of flux ~
Coming into being and dissolving
At such a speed
That it is imperceptible.
This is the subtle nature of time
Of which no one is really aware.

43 Just as a burning flame
Is not the same flame
From moment to moment;
Just as a stream of water
Flowing constantly
Is not the same water;
Just as the fruit of a tree
Is not the same fruit

At each season;
So from moment to moment
All bodies are transformed by time.

44 The foolish,
Who think it is the same flame
That burns constantly,
The same water
That always flows
In the river,
Also waste away their lives,
Thinking of the body as their sole identity.

45 Nothing is born,
Nothing dies and nothing acts.
Yet through illusion
Birth, action and death
Appear to be a reality ~
Just as it seems
That when the log has burnt out
Fire has died.

46 The body knows nine ages:
Conception, gestation, birth,
Childhood, youth, adulthood,
Maturity, old age and death.

47 These states of the body ~
Whether high or low ~
Become the sole identification.
But some, with great effort,
Give up this false identification.

48 You infer you will die
Because your father died.
You infer you were born
When you witness
Your child being born.
The Self which witnesses both
Is subject to neither.

49 One who plants a seed
And witnesses its growth,
Transformation and death,
Remains distinct from the plant ~
And from its birth, growth and death.
So it is with the Self.

50 The ignorant,
Who fail to distinguish the Self
From its appearance as matter,
Get lost in the world
Of appearances
And go from birth to death
To birth again and again.

51 Set on a course by the actions of a lifetime,
A person will take birth as a sage or god,
If those actions were sattvic in nature;
As an angel or human
If those actions were rajasic;
And as a ghoul or beast
If those actions were tamasic.

52 Just as someone
Watching others singing and dancing
Begins to sing and dance,
So the Self, even though actionless,
Appears to take on the identity
Of that seen through the awareness.

53 Just as the trees
Alongside moving water
Also seem to move,
Just as to one who has been spinning
The earth seems to spin
When they stand still;
The movement of the manifest
Appears to move the Self.

54 O Uddhava,
Descendant of Dasarha,

Just as fantasies and dreams
Are not considered real,
Neither does the Self
See manifest creation as real.

55 Yet though this manifest world is unreal,
For one committed to the senses
It never ends
And its troubles come and go,
As in dreams.

56 Therefore Uddhava,
I exhort you,
Give up this world of multiplicities
Experienced through the senses,
And see the idea of a duality
As nothing more than an illusion.

57 Even if insulted by ignoble people,
Ridiculed, envied or beaten,
Imprisoned or deprived of a livelihood,

58 Even if spat on or defiled,
By the foolish and the ignorant,
One who seeks the highest in life ~
Which is knowledge of the Self ~
Should rise above all of these
And discover the Self
Through the Self.

59 The devotee Uddhava said,

Among all teachers
You are the best.
Please explain something to me.

60 To be insulted by those who are ignorant
Seems the most difficult thing to endure.
However, those that are devoted to you
And practice all that you have taught
Seem able to endure such insult.
How is this?

Uddhava ended the last dialogue by asking a question that has troubled everyone at one time or another. Why is it so hard when people who do not approve of us voice their disapproval?

Krishna responds with the story of a wealthy man who was reduced to poverty. There are echoes here of the story of the prostitute, Pingala. Both had lived a life dedicated to pursuing happiness in something external to themselves, both arrived at a point of complete despair, and both then turned that despair into a pursuit of the Self.

The song of the miser-turned-mendicant queries the ways in which we blame our miseries on something external ~ from the stars we were born under, to other people, to our own unfortunate nature. His song takes us back to ourselves and the quest for the Self as the only true source of unending bliss.

> [1] Blessed Shuka took up the story,
>
> Being asked this question
> By his great devotee Uddhava,
> Krishna, the Bestower of Liberation,
> The Jewel of the Dasarhas,
> Answered.
>
> [2] The Radiant One, Krishna, said,
>
> Disciple of the sage Brihaspati,
> There is hardly anyone
> Who can keep an even mind
> When spoken to harshly.
>
> [3] Not even arrows
> Piercing the flesh
> And wounding the heart
> Inflict as deep a wound
> As words harshly spoken.
>
> [4] My dear Uddhava,
> There is a wonderful story
> That relates to this very subject.

Listen to it well
For it is inspiring.

5 It is a story about a sannyasin
Who was tormented by the wicked
But bore it with determined fortitude,
For these things are nothing more
Than the outcome of events long past.

6 In the country of Avanti[1]
There lived a certain wealthy brahmin
Surrounded by great luxury ~
Yet he was a miser.
Involved in the businesses
That were the source of his wealth,
He was impatient and often angry with others.

7 His home was devoid of love,
And he extended generosity
Towards no one ~
Not even himself.

8 He was so unkind and miserly
That no one loved him,
Not even his wife and children.
Neither did his servants
Feel affection for their master.

9 His only pleasure
Was in amassing wealth.
The cultivation of virtues
Never entered his mind.
The satisfaction of desires
Other than making money
Never occurred to him.
Thus the gods that preside
Over the family rites of sacrifice,
And who bestow wealth,
Grew angry with him.

10 O generous Uddhava,
As soon as his store of merit was complete,

His wealth, which he had been at pains to hoard,
Also disappeared.

11 Some of this unworthy brahmin's wealth
Was taken by his relatives,
Some by thieves;
Some he lost through poor investment,
And the rest through taxes.

12 Once his wealth was gone
And everyone, even his family,
Ignored him,
He began to worry.
Suddenly he contemplated the future
And his complete lack of virtue
Or any kind of fulfillment
That human relations bring.

13 Without money
And in desperate straits,
He became choked with remorse
And a deep distaste for the world.

14 The brahmin said to himself,

"What a sorry fool I am ~
I have deprived myself
Of both virtue and fulfillment
In this mad search for wealth.

15 "Wealth can never bring happiness
To misers
During their lifetime.
Amassing wealth torments them;
In death,
It paves the way to hell.

16 "However good one's reputation
And however virtuous one is,
Even the smallest hint of greed
Is sufficient to destroy both ~
As even the smallest mark of leprosy
Makes the most beautiful face seem ugly.

17 "Through the acquisition, increase,
Maintenance, protection
And even through the expenditure of wealth,
Everyone endures fear, anxiety and delusion.

18 "Theft, violence, lying and cheating,
Anger, quarrelsomeness, arrogance and pride,
Ostentation, enmity, distaste and rivalry,
Lust, intoxication and gambling ~

19 "These fifteen human weaknesses
Are inherent in the pursuit of wealth.
Therefore anyone seeking
The well-being of the Self
Should avoid accumulating wealth.

20 "Wives and husbands,
Fathers and mothers,
Friends and family,
All those who are dear
Will be forfeit
In the drive for wealth.

21 "Even a moderate amount of wealth
Will cause others to become envious
And behave like thieves and killers.

22 "Those who have attained a human birth,
Which even the gods of heaven desire,
And who furthermore are brahmins,
The most blessed among the initiated,
Should not ignore their own self-interest ~
Which is knowledge of the Self:
Otherwise they will meet an inauspicious end.

23 "Having attained a human body,
Which is the doorway to the final beatitude,
Who would squander it
In a quest for wealth
That can lead only to destruction?

24 "Like a demon that cares
Only for itself,
Anyone who hoards money,
Who neither propitiates the gods,
Nor makes offerings to the ancestors
And the seers and saintly sages,
Who does not share that wealth
With relatives and friends,
Who does not provide for the community ~
Surely succumbs to perdition.

25 "I have squandered my wealth,
My youth and my strength.
All that a careful person uses
To attain the highest,
I have carelessly wasted
In the search for wealth.
What can I possibly achieve
Now that I am old?

26 "How is it that even the learned
Are trapped in the snare of wealth?
There must be some illusory power
At work here.

27 "What remains for someone
Already being devoured by death?
How would riches serve me now?
How would pleasure
And the things that provide pleasure
Serve me now?
Indeed how would any action ~
Which can lead only to rebirth ~
Be of use to me now?

28 "Ah, surely the Radiant Hari,
Who embodies all the gods,
Is pleased with me
And has brought me to this despair:
For it will be the raft

By which I cross this ocean
And discover the Self.

29 "If there is any life left for me
I will dedicate it to seeking the Self,
And only to that
Which strengthens this search.

30 "May all the gods
Who rule heaven, earth
And the space between
Bear witness to this
And shower me with grace.
May I be as fortunate as King Khatvanga,[2]
Who reached heaven
In a matter of minutes."

31 The Radiant One, Krishna, continued,

Having made this resolution
The brahmin turned away from the world,
And loosened the knots
That bound his heart and hid the Self,
And became a wandering sannyasin.

32 With mind, body and vitality
All under control
This mendicant wandered the world
Entering towns and villages
Where no one knew who he was.

33 Seeing this aged and unkempt beggar
Roaming through their streets,
People mocked and ill-treated him
In every way they could think of.

34 Some snatched his bamboo staff,
Others took his begging bowl,
Yet others stole his water pot.
His rudraksha mala was taken
And his simple grass mat.
They even stole the rags he wore.

35 When he repaired to the river
To eat the little food he had begged,
They would grab it and run away.

36 Then they would tease him
With his own things ~
Pretending to offer them back
Only to snatch them away again.
People spat at him,
Some even urinated on him.
By beating him,
They forced him to speak
When he wished to be silent.

37 They used all manner of insults to taunt him:
"He is actually a rogue pretending to be a monk.
He is a thief, we must restrain him.
Quick, tie him up!"

38 Others would say,
"He is just a man deserted by his family and friends
Who has taken up the begging bowl
To get things from others."

39 Others would ridicule him by saying
"This fellow is as strong as an ox.
He keeps this silence
Simply to get something out of us."

40 They would tie him up
And heap insult upon insult,
Binding and playing with him
As if they had caught a wild bird.

41 But the brahmin knew
That his torment at the hands of others
And the suffering brought on by nature
Or even by his own body
Were not to be avoided ~
They had been given to him.

42 None of it dissuaded him
From his chosen path.

Keeping his mind in a sattvic state
He sang a song.

43 The initiated one sang,

"Neither these people,
Nor my own body,
Nor the gods,
Nor the planets,
Nor my past deeds,
Nor time,
Are the cause of my joy or distress.
All the scriptures tell me
It is my mind and my mind alone
That sets in motion
This wheel of material existence.

44 "It is this powerful mind
That activates the three gunas,
Through attachment and aversion,
From which is born action ~
Whether it be sattvic, rajasic or tamasic.
From there we begin
Walking the road of birth and death,
Orientated by the kind of action
In which we indulged.

45 "The supreme and transcendent Self
Remains aware but not involved
With the struggling mind.
That Self is the only true friend ~
Ever enlightened
It bears witness,
While the manifest Self,
Having embraced the mind
That reflects the world of objects,
Becomes bound to it.

46 "Truly the only way out
Of this dire predicament
Is the practice of generosity,
Observance of one's duties

As well as the yama and the niyama,
Listening to the Vedas,
Good works and controlling the mind.
These are indeed the highest Yoga
That lead to the ultimate goal.

47 "Some will ask,
'What is the use
Of acts of kindness and charity
To one whose mind is already controlled?'
Or, 'What else is there
To be achieved
By one whose mind is already controlled?'

48 "The senses
And even the demigods presiding over them
Are all under the control of the mind.
But the mind is more powerful
Than even the most powerful,
Seems never to come under the control
Of anyone or anything.
Therefore only by bringing the mind under control
Can the senses be controlled.

49 "Unable to conquer
This formidable foe called mind,
Whose urges tear us apart
To the very depths of our being,
People begin to evaluate this world
In terms of friends and enemies.
They will even go to war
At the urging of the mind.

50 "This body,
Which is a production of the mind,
Becomes their sole identification:
'I' and 'mine' seem different
From that which is another.
Thus deluded,
They stumble about
In a world of utter darkness.

51 "Even if other people are the cause
Of my happiness or distress,
Of what concern can that be to the Self,
Which is the Self of all people?
It is the bodies interacting here
That are the cause of both pleasure and pain ~
The Self is neither happy nor unhappy.
For if a man were to bite his own tongue
With which should he get angry ~
The tongue or the teeth?

52 "If the gods are the cause of our pain,
This still has nothing to do with the Self.
If the presiding deity of both hands is the same
And one hand strikes the other,
With which hand should the deity be angry?

53 "What if it is the Self
That is the cause of pleasure and pain?
This would mean
That both pleasure and pain
Are the essence of the Self ~
For there is nothing
Other than the Self.
The Vedas say
Everything else is an illusion ~
So there is no 'other'
To experience the pleasure and the pain.

54 "If the planets one is born under
Account for our pleasure and pain,
What has that to do with the birthless Self?
They can influence only that which is born.
Astrologers declare that these planets
Act upon each other and upon the body ~
They do not speak of them acting upon the Self.
So who should one blame,
The planets or the body for being born?

55 "If we assume that past actions
Account for our pleasure and pain

Then let it be so.
But what has this to do with the Self?
Action only arises when there is an agency
That is aware of itself and of the body.
The body without this agency cannot act,
And the agency itself is without cause and effect.
Therefore action neither is, nor does it bear fruit.
What is there to blame in this?

56 "If time is the cause of my pleasure and pain,
How does this affect the Self ~ which is time?
Since a single flame is not distressed by the whole fire
Any more than a hailstorm is distressed by the cold,
With what should I be angry?

57 "This idea-of-'I'
Creates a world,
Which it believes exists outside itself,
Bestowing pleasure and pain.
The Self is never involved in this fantasy.
One who knows this
Is free from pleasure and from pain.

58 "So just like the sages of old,
I shall give myself in devotion
To the supreme Self of all.
I shall worship at the lotus-feet
Of this Self
And in so doing I shall cross over
This ocean of darkness."

59 The Radiant One, Krishna, said,

This was the song
Sung by the monk
Who had lost his wealth
And his faith in the world;
Who wandered the earth
With nothing to call his own,
And yet was set upon
By those who envied him.
This was the song

Sung by the monk
Who remained ever free
From all fear and anxiety.

60 This world of friends and enemies
And those who are neither,
With its opposites
Of pleasure and pain,
Is truly a fantasy of the mind.
It is born of ignorance
And nothing else.

61 Therefore, my dear friend,
Control your mind
By fixing it on me.
This is the essence of Yoga.

62 One who listens to
Or repeats
This song of the monk
Will never again
Be overpowered
By the pairs of opposites.

The word Samkhya, which Krishna uses to describe the teaching in this dialogue, means "the count." Here Krishna enumerates "the many" that make up all forms and bodies. After this construction of the Universe, he goes on to provide a remarkable deconstruction back to the One. In so doing, Krishna bridges the divergent philosophical traditions of dvaita, advaita and vishishtadvaita.

What Krishna presents here is not a blind universe impelled by forces outside itself but rather an homogeneous creation moving with purpose. Brahman (which literally means "expansion") is this universe and that which transcends it. And it is with Brahman that Krishna identifies himself. Though we and the universe may appear to be participating with ~ but separate from ~ Brahman, Krishna tells us that this is not so: we are all Brahman.

This is very different from our usual view of cosmology and of ourselves. Krishna reminds us that we are not the sophisticated machines we have come to see ourselves as in this technological age. Rather, we are Brahman in the evolution and expansion of creation.

When René Descartes gave the West dualism and presented the mind as nebulous and separate from the body, we became equated with only the body, which in turn became equated with the machine. In the 1930s, Gilbert Ryle dismissed the dualism of "the ghost in the machine."[1] Krishna completes the picture in this dialogue: there is no ghost because there is no machine ~ there is the vibrant purpose-filled creation that is Brahman.

[1] The Radiant One, Krishna, said,

Let me tell you now
Of the age-old system of Samkhya
Taught by the ancients.
Through understanding it
One easily goes beyond
The idea of duality.

² During the time of the great dissolution
Before the four yugas began to run their course,
And even in the time of the first yuga,
When people possessed
True understanding,
The knower and the known
Were as one ~
An undifferentiated state of being.

³ The one absolute homogeneous Truth,
Which is beyond both mind and speech,
Through the power of maya
Becomes two:
The knower and that which is known.

⁴ These two are Purusha and Prakriti.
Prakriti can be said to have a dual nature ~
It is the unmanifest state
And the manifest state
Of all matter.
Purusha is one state
Of pure consciousness.

⁵ In order to fulfill the desires
Of the Jivas of the past
I agitated Prakriti
With my gaze,
And the gunas ~
Sattva, rajas and tamas ~ emerged.

⁶ From them
Came the first transformation:
The power of action.
With that came the other:
The power of intelligence.
From these came the ahamkara ~
The idea-of-"I":
That great bewilderer
Which itself knows not
Whether it is

The eternal conscious Self
Or the temporary unconscious body.

7 This ahamkara itself is threefold:
The sattvic mind given to goodness,
The rajasic mind given to passion,
And the tamasic mind given to ignorance.
From these three came
The subtle forms of the senses,
The senses themselves,
And the mind ~
And these enveloped
Both consciousness and matter.

8 From the tamasic vibration of the ahamkara
Came the five:
Earth, water, fire, air and space.
From the rajasic vibration of the ahamkara
Came the organs of action like the hands and feet.
From the sattvic vibration of the ahamkara
Came the presiding deities:
Vayu, who presides over the wind,
Agni, who presides over the sun,
Varuna, who presides over water,
Indra, who presides over paradise,
Upendra, who presides with Indra,
The ashvins who preside over agriculture,
Mitra who presides over friendship,
Chandra who presides over procreation
And Brahma who presides over creation.
Also from the sattvic vibration came the mind.

9 Impelled by me,
The Self of all beings,
These elements entered into each other
In perfect harmony
To become the embryo of the universe,
My residence.

10 Within that embryo I remained
Floating within the universal amniotic ocean,

And then from my naval emerged
The lotus known as the universe ~
With the self-born Brahma
Manifest in its center.

11 Through my grace,
And by the power of rajas,
And his own austerities,
Brahma, the creator, brought into being
The three spheres:
Bhurloka the earthly sphere,
Bhuvarloka the sphere of space and
Svarloka the heavenly sphere.

12 Svarloka became the abode of the gods,
Bhuvarloka became the abode of spirits
And Bhurloka the abode of people and
Other living and embodied beings.
The spheres that exist beyond Svarloka
Are the dwelling place of the perfected ones.

13 Brahma the creator
Made the subterranean region of Bhurloka
The home of demons and serpent demons.
In all these three spheres
Destinies are worked through
According to the three gunas.

14 Maharloka, Janaloka, Tapoloka and Satyaloka,
The four spheres beyond these three,
Are reached only by those
Who practice Yoga
Or do great austerities,
Or by great renunciates.
Those who practice bhakti
Come directly to my abode.

15 I am the ruler of time
Through which
The consequences of all actions taken
Must be resolved ~
Sometimes rising

To the sublime height of Satyaloka,
Sometimes sinking back down
To an earthly living existence
And the stream of the three gunas.

16 Whatever comes into being ~
Both the small and the great,
Both the narrow and the wide ~
Everything is both
Purusha and Prakriti.

17 But remember, remember:
Whatever a thing is in the beginning,
It returns to being in the end ~
That is its reality
Even in the middle.
A gold ring is always gold
Even when it ceases being a ring,
And a clay cup is always clay
Even when it has ceased being a cup.
Gold and clay are always
Their own true nature.

18 Everything that takes form,
Whether visible or invisible,
Will have an origin,
And as it is transformed
Will become the next thing ~
Like earthen clay
Transforming into a cup:
The state in which it is a cup
Has only a relative reality,
But the clay earth
Is its original and final reality.

19 Prakriti which produces matter
And provides its ingredients,
And Purusha which is the foundation,
And time which runs through it,
I am in truth all three!
For I am Brahman.

20 I alone am the ultimate cause
And by me all beings are brought into being.
From me flows creation
And through me it continues to exist
In great abundance
From generation to generation,
Until the end.

21 Finally this creation,
Which is pervaded by me as time,
This scene of endless births and deaths
Together with all the spheres of creation,
Becomes ready to return to its original state
And the dissolution begins.

22 Then the bodies of all living beings
Will dissolve to become food,
Food will dissolve into its seed,
And the seeds will merge into the earth.
Then the earth will dissolve
Into its subtle state ~ smell.

23 Smell will merge into water,
Which will merge into its subtle state ~ taste,
Which will merge into fire;
Fire will merge into its subtle state ~ the sight of form.

24 That sight will merge into air,
Which will merge into its subtle state ~ touch,
Which will merge into space,
Which will merge into its subtle state ~ hearing.
The senses will merge
Into their own subtle state ~ the gods.

25 My dear friend Uddhava,
These gods merge into the mind
And the mind into the sattvic ahamkara
Where it abides as goodness.
Sound will merge into the tamasic ahamkara
Where it abides as ignorance.
And the rajasic ahamkara,

The most powerful part of that idea-of-"I,"
Will merge into the Cosmic Intelligence.

²⁶ The Cosmic Intelligence
Merges into its own three gunas,
Which then merge
Into the unmanifest part
Of Prakriti,
Which merges into time.

²⁷ Time dissolves back into the original Jiva,
The activating principle of creation,
Which dissolves into the one supreme Being ~
Unborn, unmanifest, absolute ~
Where all things come to rest.

²⁸ Just as the rising sun
Dispels the darkness of night,
So this knowledge
Of the dissolution of all things
Dispels that ignorance
In which one sees oneself
As separate from the other.

²⁹ Thus have I ~
Witness of both consciousness and matter ~
Given you the knowledge of Samkhya,
Which ends all doubts.

In this dialogue, Krishna analyzes the different types in the human family, and shows how the gunas react with each other and on us. Here Krishna is the guru holding up a mirror in which we may see where we are on the path towards enlightenment. It is always difficult for seekers to look into that mirror, unless we hold in our awareness the love with which it is held.

If everything in this world of matter, both physical and metaphysical, is in a constant state of change ~ rajas ~ then the opposite of that ~ tamas ~ must also be present: transformation and conservation existing side by side. Of the three gunas, only sattva can be said to be weightless and motionless. The opposites of sattva are tamas (mass) and rajas (motion). Neither sattva nor tamas will anything new into creation ~ will characterizes rajas (movement, energy) alone.

The three gunas are found in everything in creation and yet they do not mix and blend but react with each other. Each seeks dominance over the others. In the darkness of night, day will begin its ascendancy and vice versa. We sleep and awaken to renewed energy and activity. After a day's activity, we are overcome by sleep. Throughout our lives, everything we touch, everything we eat, everything we do, will be governed by the gunas, our three constant companions.

Here Krishna advises us on how to overcome them all: how to subordinate tamas to rajas and rajas to sattva through devotional practice, and then how to transcend all three. For it is only beyond the reach of the gunas that we can experience the Self beyond all multiplicities and dissolve into Oneness.

> [1] The Radiant One, Krishna, spoke again,
>
> O best among men,
> Listen to me now as I explain
> The effect each guna
> Has on a person.
>
> [2] Control of the mind
> And control of the senses,

Tolerance and perception,
Practicing the austerities
Inherent in one's own duty,
Truthfulness and compassion,
Mindfulness and contentment,
Generosity and dispassion,
Shame for wrongs done,
Faith accompanied by
Charity, modesty and simplicity,
And turning one's vision inward
To the Self.

3 Desire for material gain,
Impulsive action,
Presumption and arrogance,
Restlessness and dissatisfaction,
Praying always for an outcome,
Taking the separatist view,
Gratification of the senses,
Courage born of intoxication,
A fondness for praise and fame,
Ridiculing others and
Aggressive independence.

4 Intolerance and miserliness,
Cheating and other falsehoods,
Hatred and enmity,
Importunity and hypocrisy,
Languor and destructiveness,
Anguish and delusion,
False humility,
Laziness and expectations,
Fear and timidity.

5 These are the effects
Of sattva, rajas and tamas respectively.
Now hear of their effects
When they react with one another.

6 O Uddhava,
Ideas-of-"I" and -"mine" are a direct result

Of the synthesis of the three gunas.
All interaction with this world,
Which is mediated through the mind,
The senses, the means of action
And the prana,
Is the result of a reaction
Of the gunas with each other.

7 When a person
Is keenly devoted to religious merit,
The acquisition of wealth
And the gratification of desires,
This is also a result of the three gunas
Reacting with each other:
It is they that are contributing to faith,
Prosperity and attachment.

8 In the person wholly devoted to religious rites
In order to gain a purpose,
And who rigorously keeps to the householder's life
In order to gain riches,
This is said to be a result of the three gunas
Reacting with each other.

9 In those imbued with self-control
Sattva predominates.
In those imbued with desire
Rajas predominates.
In those imbued with anger
Tamas predominates.

10 Anyone, man or woman,
Who worships me with loving devotion
Devoid of desire for gain,
Can be understood to be
Of a sattvic temperament.

11 But when they worship me ~
Even though it be through their own duties ~
With a motive of gain in mind,
Then they can be understood to be

Of a rajasic temperament.
And those who worship me
With the intention of bringing harm to others,
Can be understood to be
Of a tamasic temperament.

12 These three gunas
Have no effect on the supreme Self,
But they do affect the individual awareness.
Through the mind they entice the awareness
To become attached to the body
And worldly objects.
This constitutes individual bondage.

13 When sattva, which is bright and pure
And filled with auspiciousness,
Predominates over rajas and tamas,
The individual becomes possessed of joy,
Virtue and knowledge.

14 When rajas, which gives rise to attachment,
Passion and the illusion of multiplicities,
Overcomes both sattva and tamas,
The individual is seized with a desire
For fame and fortune,
And attended by unhappiness and struggle.

15 When tamas, which clouds one's judgment,
Veils one's vision and gives rise to dullness,
Overcomes both rajas and sattva,
The individual becomes lethargic and belligerent,
And always expects unreasonable help from others.

16 When there is clarity of mind,
Stillness of the senses,
And fearlessness,
Then understand
You are in the mode of sattva ~
In which Self-realization is possible.

17 When the mind has become active
And clouds the consciousness

Through restlessness of the body and the senses,
Then understand
You are in the mode of rajas.

18 When the mind becomes lethargic,
Depressed and dull
And unable to reflect on the Self,
Then understand
You are in the mode of tamas.

19 When in the individual
Sattva is ascendant,
Know that the divine is strengthened.
When in the individual
Rajas is ascendant,
Know that the demonic is strengthened.
When in the individual
Tamas is ascendant,
Know that ignorance is strengthened.

20 From a sattvic state
One can expect wakefulness
In the individual.
From a rajasic state
One can expect dreaminess
In the individual.
From a tamasic state
One can expect sleepiness
In the individual.

21 Those who follow the conduct
Prescribed in the Vedas
Go to higher and higher states of sattva.
Those who follow the path
Of ignorance ~ of tamas ~
Go to states that are lower and lower.
Those who follow the path
Of passion ~ of rajas ~
Continue to go between high and low.

22 Those who die in a state of sattva
Ascend to the heavenly realms.

Those who die in a state of rajas
Return to earth in human form.
Those who die in a state of tamas
Descend to the dark regions.
Those who have transcended
These three states of
Rajas, tamas and sattva
Are absorbed into me.

23 Action performed as an offering to me
Without expectations of results
Is indeed sattvic action.
Action performed with a desire
To enjoy results
Is indeed rajasic action.
Action performed through enmity and envy
Is indeed tamasic action.

24 Knowledge of the Absolute is sattvic.
Knowledge of duality is rajasic.
The absence of knowledge is tamasic.
Knowledge of me
Is beyond these three.

25 The forest is sattvic,
The city is rajasic
And the gambling dens are tamasic.
My dwelling place in the temples
Is beyond these three.

26 One who works free from attachment
Call such a one a sattvika.
One who works for personal gain
Call such a one a rajasa.
One who works without knowing right from wrong
Call such a one a tamasa.
But one who works taking refuge in me,
Is beyond these three.

27 Faith in the spiritual path is sattvic.
Faith in the outcome of labor is rajasic.

Faith in ignorance and dullness is tamasic.
Faith in devotion to me
Is beyond these three gunas.

28 Food that is wholesome, pure
And easily prepared is sattvic.
Food that agitates the sense of taste
Is rajasic.
Food that is impure and unclean
Is tamasic.

29 Joy that springs from the Self is sattvic.
Joy that arises from the senses is rajasic.
Joy that emanates from ignorance is tamasic.
Joy from experiencing me
Is beyond these three.

30 Objects, places, outcomes, time,
Knowledge, actions, doers, faith,
State of awareness, form and goal,
All come under the domain
Of the gunas.

31 O best among men, understand:
Without exception
Everything that emanates
From Purusha and Prakriti,
Whether seen, heard or only thought of,
Comes under the domain
Of these three gunas.

32 Gentle Uddhava,
The cycle of birth and death and birth again
Is nothing but the flow of the gunas,
Which are themselves the product of the mind.
One who overcomes them
Through the path of devotion to me
Is absorbed into me.

33 Let the wise,
Having attained this longed-for human body,
Which is so disposed towards liberation,

Free themselves from attachment to these *gunas*
And through devotion come to me.

34 Free from attachment
And with the senses under control,
The wise should worship me
With affectionate awareness
And thus overcome rajas and tamas with sattva.

35 With the mind thus calmed
Overcome even sattva
Through continued dispassion
Towards the material world.
Thus the wise overcome all three gunas,
Release themselves from the idea-of-"I,"
And fix their attention on the absolute Self.

36 Such a being ~
Who is freed from matter and energy,
The visible and the invisible,
And the three gunas;
And who from inside or outside
Needs nothing
And desires nothing ~
Becomes wholly fulfilled by Brahman.

Pingala the prostitute and the avaricious merchant were both given the opportunity to look at their lives and take a different direction. Dialogue 21 tells a similar story, about a king who had become infatuated with the celestial nymph Urvashi. The nymph had warned the king not to become attached to her as she would one day leave him. When she does, the king is devastated and then transformed. Each of these protagonists, from the prostitute to the king, has a song about their life and the circumstances that brought them to the point of revelation.

We all have a song ~ but are we singing it? I find it interesting that Krishna says not that they tell their stories but that they sing them. Singing requires a different voice; a certain tone and pitch beyond the one we usually use. A song is not like a story ~ it does not simply describe an episode but is the whole legend of the person. Each of us is striving towards the singing of our own song. And, as in these three lives, we may only find that song in our darkest moments: for only those moments can force us into the light of a new awareness.

This dialogue looks again at the effect of our associations. The mind does not act independently but is colored by the world around it. If we keep company with those who seek only what this world has to offer, that is what we too will seek. Krishna advises that if you wish to find the Self, keep company with those who are making that journey too.

[1] The Radiant One, Krishna, said,

Having taken a human form,
Which is a reflection
Of the supreme and blissful Self
Situated in the heart of all,
Realize me through devotion.

[2] Transcending the gunas,
One who is completely free
Ceases to identify with an individuality
That has been established in this world.

Such a one sees this world
For the illusion it is ~
An apparition that is not real,
Living and yet not living.
While in this world
The wise do not get entangled with it.

3 Do not associate with the unwise ~
Those who seek only to satisfy
Their passion and their hunger.
If you do
You will fall into the darkest pit ~
The blind following the blind.

4 Let me tell you the song
That King Pururavas sang
When he came to his senses
From being distraught
After his wife Urvashi
Had left him.¹

5 When Urvashi left the emperor,
Though naked he ran after her,
Yelling like one possessed,
"You are my wife, stay,
Do not be cruel,
Stay, please stay."

6 For many years he had enjoyed
The pleasures of her body ~
Not even noticing
When nights passed into days.
Still he wanted her and
Hungered for her.

7 King Pururavas sang,

"My infatuation has had a powerful hold of me.
For years I was in the grip of this goddess,
Not even noticing that my life was passing by.

8 "Besotted by her
I did not see the sun set;

Nor did I see it rise.
Days numbering years
Have passed away.

9 "Where was the power
Of my sovereignty
When I ran after this woman
Like a common cur
As she left me so coolly?

10 "Here I am, king of kings,
And she walked away
As if I were of no more consequence
Than a humble blade of grass.
Yet naked and without shame
I ran after her, begging her to return.

11 "Will courage, influence and power
Stay with me now,
Even though I have degraded myself
Before this woman who has deserted me?

12 "Of what use is education,
Renunciation, austerities
And religious rituals,
Or the years of living
In solitude and silence,
When one's mind
Can become so captivated
By a beautiful woman?

13 "Woe to me!
I achieved a kingship
And thought I was above it all,
But I was just another fool ~
Ignorant of my own welfare.
I was a king a woman conquered,
And led like an ass with a ring through its nose.

14 "Though for many years
I had drunk the nectar of her lips
Again and again, my passion for Urvashi

Arose in my body and in my mind ~
Like a fire being fed with oblations.

15 "Who but the supreme One,
That lies beyond this world
And is the object of desire
Of saints and sages,
Will save me now
From the clutches of this whore?

16 "O no! I was the fool ~
I was the slave to my own senses,
For this goddess Urvashi warned me
With wise words
That I never listened to.

17 "I cannot blame her ~
I was the one enslaved.
Does a rope lying on the ground
Bite the man who thinks it is a snake?

18 "O this polluted body,
Destined for the foul odors of decay!
It was I who was distracted
By the fragrance and beauty of a woman
When that beauty
Was but an illusory sheath.

19 "To whom does this body belong?
Is it to the parents who brought it into the world?
Or is it to the wife who gives it pleasure?
Or perhaps it is to the master who orders it around?
Or maybe it belongs to the flames of the funeral pyre
Or the dogs and jackals who devour it?
Or is it one's friends and relatives that can claim it?
Or is it the Self?
Who knows?

20 "We know who ultimately owns this body
And yet we become so attached to it.
Destined for a lowly end, this body yet
Sees a pretty face and is immediately enchanted:

'What beauty. What a charming nose,
What beautiful eyes.'

21 "What is the difference between this body ~
Composed of skin, flesh, blood, sinew,
Fat marrow and bone,
And filled with urine and excrement ~
And a body full of maggots?

22 "Truly, even the wise man would do well
To stay clear of beautiful women.
For the mind is agitated
Only when the senses are stimulated
By being close to the object of desire.

23 "The mind is not disturbed
By that which it neither sees nor hears.
Therefore the mind of one
Who controls the senses
Is gradually calmed
And finally attains peace.

24 "There should be
No sensual associations
With women or with
Men who lust after women.
If even the wise do not trust their passions
Why should a man like me?"

25 The Radiant One, Krishna, said,

Having thus sung his song,
Pururavas, king of kings,
Famous even among the gods,
Gave up seeking Urvashi's domain.
Cleansed of his infatuation
He attained transcendent knowledge,
And realizing me as the Self
In the depths of his own heart,
At last he experienced peace.

26 One who craves wisdom
Should avoid the company of the unwise

And seek association with the wise:
For it is their words that will sever
The attachments of the mind.

27 These saints wander through this world
Yet are independent of it.
They have a calm disposition,
And are beyond the pairs of opposites
Like pleasure and pain;
They reject the world's inducements
And know that the idea-of-"I" is false.

28 O lucky Uddhava,
In the company of the wise
There is talk only of the Self.
Listening to these people,
Purged of their sins,
One overcomes all illusions.

29 Those who reverently listen
To this chant of King Pururavas,
Who listen to the discussions of the wise,
Become attached to me
And grow in faith and devotion.

30 What more remains to be accomplished
By one who is devoted to me?
I am that Brahman ~
The Infinite,
And the absolute Bliss.

31 Just as one who approaches a fire
Need no longer fear the cold or the dark,
So it is for anyone
Who approaches the saintly.

32 For all those who sink and rise
Again and again
In life's ocean of death and rebirth,
The devotees who know Brahman
Are like a lifeboat
That rescues the drowning.

33 Just as food is the life of the living,
I am the ultimate shelter for the distressed.
Just as religion is the only wealth
That the dying can claim,
For those being claimed by the ocean of samsara
My devotees are the only refuge.

34 My devotees
Will awaken the inner vision,
Just as surely as the risen sun
Grants the outer vision.
Let these saints be your deities and your family ~
They are the Self undifferentiated from me.

35 Having abandoned his attachment to Urvashi,
King Pururavas began to roam the earth
Free of all attachments
And taking pleasure in the Self alone.

✳ *Dialogue 22*

In this dialogue, Krishna continues to challenge formal ritual, placing the ghee of the Vedic fire ceremony alongside the offerings of water, fruit, flowers and perfumes used in the puja before the ishta devata (the chosen deity). Doing so gave simple personal devotion equal status to the formalized ritual of the Vedas. In the spirit of Hinduism, these new forms of worship were to become incorporated into the whole (in Verse 31, for example, Krishna tells his devotees to chant Vedic hymns during the new puja). The priesthood in India was never wiped out but instead assimilated new practices such as bhakti.

This social history is not dissimilar from the individual history of a spiritual seeker. At the beginning of the journey, we often perform rites and rituals through the medium of someone else and accept the authority of others in our relationship with Brahman. But there comes a time when the intermediary must step back to allow us to conduct a more direct relationship with the chosen deity. Only then will we discover the Brahman that is transcendent and beyond comprehension as well as the Brahman that is immediate and immanent.

Some of the rituals that Krishna gives here are simple, others are complex and intricate. He leaves it to us to choose what is appropriate:

[1] The devotee Uddhava said,

Adored One, please explain to me
How to worship you through ceremony.
Tell me also who worships you thus
And for what purpose.

[2] Great sages like Narada,[1]
The divine Vyasa and even Brihaspati,
Son of Angira and teacher of the gods,
Have said that such ceremonial worship
Is the highway to goodness and liberation.

[3] I know that the instructions for such ceremonies
Came first from your lips
To the ear of Brahma the creator,
Who told it to his sons ~ Bhrigu and the others.

The Great One, Shiva, having heard it from you,
Taught it to his consort, Parvati.

4 Giver of grace,
I know that the path of devotion
That can be attained through this ceremony
Is one that everyone can walk ~
Whether they are born high or low,
Man or woman.

5 O Giver of Grace,
Ruler of the Universe,
Tell me ~ your sincere devotee ~
This method of severing
The knots of karma.

6 The Radiant One, Krishna, said,

The Vedic prescriptions for such worship
Are indeed endless, O Uddhava.
So let me tell you briefly
How you may conduct
Such ceremonial worship.

7 There are three ways in which
I accept worship:
Vedic, Tantric² or a mixture of the two.
Select one of the three
And then use that.

8 Listen how one
Who has undergone initiation
May worship me
Through Vedic prescription
And with devotion.

9 With sincerity and devotion
And with the appropriate offerings
The initiated should worship me:
As the Supreme Guru,
Or the Indweller of the deity,
Or the Indweller of the sacred ground,
Or the Indweller of the sun,

Or the Indweller of water,
Or even as the Indweller
Of the worshiper's own heart.

10 First cleanse the body
By bathing it and cleaning the teeth.
Then perform a second purification with earth
While reciting the mantras
Of both the Vedas and of Tantra.

11 The Vedas say
My worship should be done
At each of the three junctures of the day,
Dawn, noon and twilight.
One should vow to undertake such worship
With a determination
To perform it in the right manner
And with the appropriate prayers.
This will destroy at the root all karma.

12 An image of me
May be made of stone, wood, metal,
Or earth such as clay,
Or sandalwood paste,
Or it may be carved from precious stones,
Or painted on a surface.
Or it may be an image
Composed in the mind.
These are the eight forms of images
Through which I may be worshiped in ceremony.

13 Dear Uddhava,
Images are the dwelling place of the divine
And can be divided into two types:
The permanent and the impermanent.
Once there has been an invocation
Inviting the presence of the divine
Into the permanent image,
It can never be dismissed.

14 Invocation for the impermanent image
Is optional unless
It is installed on sacred ground ~
Then such invocation is compulsory.
Bathing is performed with all these images
Except those made of clay, wood or sandalwood paste ~
Water may be sprinkled on these
As a token bathing.

15 Worship of an image by a sincere devotee
Should be done with the choicest offerings.
If the image is held in the heart
Then these offerings will also come from the heart.

16 When I am worshiped
In the form of an image,
Bathing and decoration are
Most dear to me.
When I am worshiped
As an image traced on sacred ground,
And my powers are established
In all the proper places
Through the recitation of mantras
And offerings of sesame and barley
Soaked in ghee, that is
Also dear to me.

17 When I am worshiped as the sun,
The meditation of the twelve asanas
And their mantras
Is most dear to me.
When I am worshiped in the form of water,
Worship me by offering that water itself.
Rest assured that whatever is offered to me
In devotion and with faith,
Is most dear to me.

18 I am not pleased by an offering ~
No matter how grand ~
That is made by one who lacks devotion.
But I am delighted

When someone filled with devotion
Offers even the smallest thing.
Imagine then, how I receive gifts
Of fragrant oils, incense, flowers and food
That are offered with love.

19 After bathing
And gathering the offerings for the ceremony,
The devotee should position a mat of sacred grass
To serve as a seat,
Placing it so that it faces either east or north;
Or if the image is permanent
It should face the image directly.

20 The devotee should sanctify
The parts of his or her body
By touching them with water
While reciting the appropriate mantras.[3]
This should also be done for
The deity being worshiped,
The jug containing the water
And the articles of worship.

21 With water from that same vessel
The devotee should sprinkle the ground
Around the deity, the offerings
And his or her own body.
Then the devotee may prepare the vessels
That will contain the water for the puja
Before filling them.

22 The worshiper should consecrate
The three vessels of water ~
For bathing the feet of the deity,
For offering in greeting
And for offering for drinking ~
By chanting into them these sacred mantras:
"Hridaya namah," the formula of the heart,
Into the vessel of water for bathing the feet;
"Shirase svaha," the formula of the head,
Into the vessel to be offered in greeting;

"Shikhayai vashat," the formula of the crown,
Into the vessel to be offered for drinking.
Then chant the Gayatri mantra to all three.

23 Then the worshiper should visualize
His own heart and the heart of the subtle body
As having been cleansed
First by wind which dries
And then by fire which burns:
These are the ancient purifiers.
Then let this empty space be filled
By the nectar that flows from the moon
Into the center of the forehead.
Then see in the heart the Supreme Form
Forever seated on a lotus.
My presence is there ~
As subtle as the final echo
Of the pranava mantra, Om.

24 Just as a lamp lights up an entire room,
The devotee should feel that my presence
Pervades the whole body,
And should then surrender
The space of the body to me.
Then with great reverence
The devotee should touch
The different parts of the image
While chanting the appropriate mantras,
And feel that the deity has also entered the image
Before which he or she is about to worship.

25 The devotee should know
That that which supports
The lotus the deity rests upon
Is made up of four legs:
Dharma, righteousness,
Jnana, wisdom,
Vairagya, dispassion,
Aishvarya, sovereignty;
And four sides that constitute their opposites:
Adharma, the absence of righteousness,

Ajnana, the absence of knowledge,
Avairagya, the absence of dispassion,
Anaishvarya, the absence of sovereignty.
The three gunas are the three base supports,
And the nine shaktis are all part of this support:
Vimala, purity,
Utkarshini, exaltation,
Jnana, knowledge,
Kriya, performance of actions,
Yoga, practices of mystical power,
Prahvi, humility,
Satya, truth,
Ishana, power, and
Anugraha, grace.
Knowing this the devotee can proceed
With the worship, and offer:

26 The water for the feet,
The water for the greeting and
The water for the mouth,
With the other articles of worship.
Through such a puja
The devotee will achieve merit
In this world and the next.

27 The devotee should also worship my weapons:
My disc, sudarshana, with which I protect the worlds;
My conch, panchajanya;
My club, my sword, my arrows and my bow.
Worship too my plow and my pestle.
And remember to worship also the three things
That rest eternally on my chest:
My celebrated jewel, the kaustubha[4] gem,
My garland and the white shrivatsa[5] symbol.

28 Also worship with welcome offerings
All those who attend me:
Nanda, Sunanda, Garuda,
Prachanda and Chanda also,
Mahabala and Bala,

Kamuda and Kumudekshana.
All these surround me
In all directions.

[29] The devotee should also worship
Through a full offering of water and a puja
The great goddess Durga and
The elephant god Vinayaka,
And the sages Vyasa and Vishvakshena.[6]
All these surround me also.

[30] According to the wealth of the devotee
The deity should be bathed in scented waters
And worshiped daily
With sandalwood paste and camphor,
With saffron, aloe wood and fragrant root.

[31] This should be done while chanting
Sacred hymns from the Vedas including
The mantras of the *Rig Veda*,
The *Sama Veda*, the Rajana Sama
As well as the Rohina Sama.[7]

[32] Then the devotee
Should decorate me with garments,
The sacred thread,
Ornaments and jewels,
The tilak[8] mark and a garland.
And then anoint my body with sacred oils.

[33] The devotee should faithfully offer to me
The water for bathing my feet and my mouth,
Fragrant oils and flowers,
Unbroken grains and incense,
And a lighted lamp.

[34] If it is within their means
The devotees may offer me
Sugar and rice with sweetened milk,
Sweet cakes made of coconut and flour,
Wheat and ghee covered in sugar and spices,
Yoghurt, vegetables and other foods.

35 On sacred days
Or even daily if possible,
The deity should be anointed
With oil and scented powders;
Presented with a mirror
And a twig which cleans the teeth;
And offered food
That can be eaten without chewing
As well as food that must be chewed.
The five kinds of nectar[9]
Should be offered for bathing,
And the deity should be entertained
With singing and dancing.

36 If the devotee is worshiping through fire,
The area should be chosen and cleared
According to Vedic injunctions.
When lighting the sacred fire
The devotee should bring it to a blaze
With wood offered with his or her own hands.

37 Then the devotee must spread
The sacred kusha grass around the fire
And sprinkle water on it.
Having placed the kindling in the fire,
While reciting the sacred mantras
Prescribed in the Vedas
The devotee can place the offerings near by
And meditate on me as the fire:

38 My complexion will be
The color of molten gold;
In my arms I will bear
The conch, the disc, the club and the lotus;
I will have a serene countenance
And wear a cloth made of lotus petals
The color of gold.

39 I will be wearing a glittering crown,
Bright bracelets and a waistband.
The shrivatsa mark will be on my chest

With the bright kaustubha gem.
And I will be wearing a garland
Made of wild flowers.

40 The offering the devotee makes
Will be firewood soaked in ghee.
The devotee should make
The two offerings of ghee known as agharas:
The ghee should be poured
From the northern to the southern end ~
And from the southern to the northern end,
Of the sacrificial fire pit
While pronouncing the proper mantras.

41 One should then continue offering into the fire
While chanting the mantras of the gods ~
Beginning with the Yamaraja.
The devotee should also chant
The sixteen-lines
Of the Purusha Shuktam,[10]
Making an offering at the end of each line.

42 Having thus worshiped
And prostrated,
The devotee should make offerings
To the associates of the deity,
Uttering for each their own particular mantra.
Then the devotee
Should engage in silent mantra
And meditate on the deity
As the supreme Self.

43 Once again the devotee
Should offer water
For bathing the feet and the mouth
And offer the remnants of the deity's food
Up to Vishvakshena.
Then the devotee should present the deity
With perfumed betel nut.

44 The devotees should sing
Hymns that honor the deity

And dance
And recount stories of the deity
To each other.
In this manner the devotees
Should remain absorbed
In the glory of the Self.

45 All kinds of hymns and prayers
Should be made into offerings
Using the ancient mantras,
And reciting prayers for mercy,
The devotee should prostrate
Before the deity.

46 Having placed his or her head
At the feet of the deity,
The devotee should stand before it
With hands in prayer:
Asking for mercy
As if standing at the jaws of death.

47 Then the devotee may receive
The remnants of the sacrifice offered,
Touching them reverently to the head.
If the image is to be removed after the ceremony
Then the devotee should once again
Place the light of the deity
Within their own heart.

48 Since I am the supreme Self of all
I will be present in whatever form
The devotee wishes to worship me ~
I am even the presence within the devotee.
I am the Self of the universe
And that which transcends this universe.

49 By worshiping me
Through this practice of Kriya Yoga,11
Which is written in the Vedas and the Tantras,
The devotee will receive the blessing of perfection
Both in this life and in the next.

⁵⁰ The devotee can ensure constant worship
By the creation of a temple
With pleasant gardens
In which flowers for puja can be grown.

⁵¹ One who worships regularly
And on special days
With gifts that are grand
Will receive a splendor
Equal to my own.

⁵² By installing the deity in a temple,
One rules the earth.
By building a temple,
One rules the three worlds.
By worshiping and serving the deity
One ascends to the sphere of Brahma;
And by doing all three,
One attains a transcendent form like my own.

⁵³ But one who engages
In these devotional ceremonies
Simply out of love for me
Without any thought of reward ~
That is the devotee
Who attains the Self.
Thus have I described
The modes of ceremonial worship.

⁵⁴ Anyone who steals
That which is meant for worship ~
Even if it was a gift
That the thief originally made ~
Such a one will live as a worm
For ten thousand times ten thousand years.

⁵⁵ Not only the thief
But any accomplice
Will share that fate
In proportion to their complicity.

❋ Dialogue 23

This dialogue contains one of the most direct teachings in the entire text. Krishna's words are more than ever to the point ~ his remaining time on earth is short and any remaining confusion must be dispelled.

I noticed that the truths that my own guru, Swami Venkatesanandaji, taught in gentle words when I first met him were said without "frills" at the end of his life. Life is short and each of us marches towards the certainty of death without the certainty of knowing when we will arrive there. We must clear up our confusion now, in the very midst of our lives. And we do so by renouncing the mythology we have built around ourselves and the world we perceive. We have to begin from that point where the only thing we can say with any conviction is, "I think I am experiencing something but I'm not quite sure what it is." It is this point at which the ahamkara most vigorously refuses co-operation, clinging fiercely to illusion as if it were a reality.

The scientist Arthur Eddington put it this way:

> Nothing is real. Not even the scientist's wife. Quantum physics leads one to the belief that his wife is a rather elaborate differential equation.... To put the conclusion crudely, the stuff of the world is mind stuff.[1]

That is it: the "stuff" of the world is mind-stuff. Only when this becomes a conviction can our spiritual enquiry begin. If we stay true to the journey, we will arrive at the vision Krishna promises us in Verse 33.

[1] The Radiant One, Krishna, said,

Understanding the essential oneness
Of Purusha and Prakriti
Helps you to avoid making judgments
About the nature and actions of others.

[2] To praise or criticize
Is simply to make a commitment
To that which is unreal.
This can only lead to a vision
That is always limited to duality.

3 When an individual
Is dreaming or sleeping deeply
He or she loses awareness of the external world.
If you see only the world of multiplicities
And do not extend your vision to the One,
You will be like the dreamer and the sleeper
And continue to encounter the illusion of death.

4 In a duality that does not really exist
What is real and what is unreal?
What is good and what is bad?
Yet making such judgments
And speaking about them
Gives them a reality in one's mind.

5 Reflections, echoes and mirages ~
Even though one knows they are unreal ~
Will cause a reaction.
Thus the body
Continues to inspire a fear of death
As long as one identifies with it.

6 The supreme Self alone is.
It is the creator and the created;
The protector and the protected;
The destroyer and the destroyed.

7 Therefore nothing other than the Self exists.
That which appears to exist,
That threefold category of
The self of each being or object,
The agency by which it exists and moves,
And the thing itself ~
All exist within the Self alone
And only appear as separate on account of maya.

8 One who knows this
And for whom
This knowledge has become reality
Neither judges nor criticizes.
Such a person

Moves about in this world
Like the sun which shines on all alike.

9 By means of one's own perception,
Reasoning or by scriptural authority,
One comes to the only conclusion
About this world that is possible:
It had a beginning and it will have an end.
Knowing this,
Move in the world
But be free of it.

10 The devotee Uddhava said,

Experiences ~ like birth and death,
Pain and pleasure ~ are experienced
Neither by the Self, which is the subject,
Nor by the body, which is the object.
Yet they seem to be experienced.
What is it then that experiences?

11 The Self is eternal, transcendent and pure ~
It is a light unto itself like fire.
The material body is like unlit firewood,
Which is incapable of light on its own.
So what is it that actually undergoes
The experience of a material life?

12 The Radiant One, Krishna, said,

As long as the Self sees itself
Through an undiscriminating intelligence
As the body, the senses and the vitality,
And limits itself to those,
This relative existence, though unreal,
Will appear to be real.

13 As long as a dream is not disturbed
All objects within it appear to be real.
Similarly, although this world of experience
Does not exist any more than a dream does,
As long as people identify with it

They will continue to undergo these experiences
Even while their true nature is transcendent to it.

14 In a dream
One may experience many disturbing things,
Yet on awakening
Cease to be disturbed by them.
Once awakened,
The previous experience causes no disturbance.

15 Emotions like sorrow and joy,
Fear, anger, greed, infatuation,
Confusion and so on,
All belong to the idea-of-"I"
That experiences birth and death ~
But not to the Self.

16 The Self hidden in the body,
The senses, the prana and the mind
Is called the Jiva.
The subtle body,
Made up of karma and the gunas,
Evolves from the primary manifestation
Known as the Cosmic Intelligence.
Ruled by time
They move through this world of samsara
As if separate.

17 The wise sage
With an intelligence sharpened
Through proper devotion to the guru
Cuts out the idea-of-"I,"
Which is the root cause
Of this world of multiplicities
And is therefore free
Even while moving through this world.

18 Wisdom is the ability
To distinguish the real from the unreal.
Such wisdom may be gained
Through study of the Vedas,

Performance of one's own duties,
Practice of austerities,
Direct perception,
Listening to historical accounts,
And simple logic.
Such wisdom will lead you to understand:
That which was at the beginning of creation,
And which will continue after creation,
Is also that which is now ~
As both the creation and its cause.

19 Just as gold,
Which exists as itself
Before being fashioned into an ornament,
Remains gold once fashioned,
Even though it may be called a bracelet,
Or an earring or a necklace,
Is still gold when the ornament is melted ~
So am I, the cause of this Universe:
I am what I am
Even when called creation.

20 My dear Uddhava,
That agency by which
The mind is subject to the three states
Of waking, dreaming and deep sleep;
The agency by which creation
Is subject to the three gunas;
And that which is the support
Of the agency by which all of creation
Appears, transforms and disappears ~
That alone is Truth.

21 That which did not exist before this creation
And which will not exist after its disappearance
Does not exist during creation either ~
To say that it does is simply empty words
Signifying nothing.
This is my conviction:
Whatever is created and revealed

By another object or being
Is nothing other than its creator and revealer.

22 Not real, it appears from rajas guna,
As the multiplicity of things including
The mind, the senses and the objects
That the senses are caught up in.
Yet all of it is nothing other
Than the Self-illuminating Brahman.

23 Remove all doubts
Through a clear understanding of Reality.
Cease to identify with the unreal
And identify yourself with the Real ~
With Brahman.
Turn away from fleeting moments of pleasure
And enjoy the constant ecstasy
Of the eternal Self.

24 This material body belongs to matter,
Not to the eternal Self.
Neither the senses,
Nor the prana, the breath you breathe,
Water, fire or mind,
The intelligence, the sensory nerves,
The idea-of-"I," space, earth,
And not even the
Original undifferentiated state of matter,
Can be considered the Self.

25 When there is complete and total
Identification with the Self,
What does it matter
If the senses,
Which are nothing more than the gunas,
Become agitated and flow outward?
What does it matter to the sun
If clouds come and go?

26 Just as space remains untouched
By air, fire, water and earth,

Or by the changing of the seasons ~
So does the Self remain untouched
By the idea-of-"I" and the flow of the gunas.

27 Nevertheless contact with the objects
To which the senses are attracted
By the illusory power of maya,
Should be firmly rejected ~
Until through devotion and practice
All passion is removed from the mind.

28 Just as a disease not properly eradicated
Will return again and again and bring pain,
So will it be with a mind
Not properly purified of desires
In a Yogi who has not attained perfection.

29 Sometimes complete realization of the Self
Is interrupted by family and friends,
Who are sent by the gods to distract the Yogi.
But on the strength of their Yoga practices
They will resume such endeavors in their next life,
And not again become trapped in the cycle
Of action and reaction.

30 Impelled by ignorance,
People engage in actions
To achieve certain ends
Until death comes upon them.
It is not so with the wise who,
Being immersed in the bliss of the Self,
Are not attracted to material gain
Even while living in this world of
Action and reaction.

31 The wise,
With their awareness fixed on the Self,
Let the body do what is natural to it:
Eating, sleeping, standing, sitting,
Walking, lying down, excreting
And all its other biological functions.

32 When those who are wise
Perceive an object of the senses,
They fully understand
That it has no existence of its own
And is nothing other than the Self.
To the wise,
The distinct nature of the object
Has no more reality
Than a fading dream
To someone waking up.

33 Dear Uddhava,
Prior to the dawning of wisdom
People identify themselves
With everything that comes
Under the domain of the gunas ~
Including all actions taken.
But by the cultivation of wisdom
Such ignorance fades,
And the Self alone remains:
Neither accepted nor rejected,
It is that which is.

34 The light of the rising sun
Destroys darkness
And reveals the world of external objects ~
But it does not create them.
In the same way
Self-realization removes the darkness
That obscures a person's consciousness.

35 The Supreme is never hidden from view.
It is self-luminous, unborn and immeasurable.
It is pure transcendent consciousness, fully aware.
It is one without a second.
It is beyond speech ~
For it is That which impels speech
And by which the vitality functions.

36 Indeed, there is no basis
For a perception of duality

In the Self ~
This is simply the product
Of a confused mind.

37 The world of seeming multiplicities
That appears through the five tattvas
As name and form
Has no reality.
Those who argue that it does,
And that Vedic passages referring to them
Should be taken literally,
Do so because they do not understand.

38 Should the body of a Yogi
Who is not yet an adept
Be overtaken by obstacles,
The following is recommended:

39 Some obstacles will be overcome
Through concentrated focus of the attention,
And others by engaging in Yogic asanas,
Together with concentration and breath control.
Yet others may be overcome through special austerities,
Mantras or even medicinal herbs.

40 More persistent obstacles may be overcome
Through meditation on me and chanting my name
Either in a group with others or alone,
And by rendering service to the great Yogis.

41 There are some who dedicate themselves
To those Yogic practices that impart
A strong body that remains youthful
And does not succumb to old age.
Their Yoga practices are aimed
At the attainment of siddhis.

42 However the wise
Know the utter futility of this endeavor
For all bodies die.
They know that the Self is to the body

As the tree is to fruit ~
One remains and the other decays.

[43] In the course of practicing Yoga
The physical body may become strong.
Yet the wise accept this
Without pinning any hope on it,
Remaining devoted only to the Self.

[44] Thus the practicing Yogi
Who takes shelter in me,
And who is without desire,
Is never overwhelmed
And attains realization of the Self.

❀ Dialogue 24

In the final dialogue of the *Uddhava Gita*, Bhagavan Shri Krishna signals the end of the teaching and Uddhava takes his leave, to follow the path his teacher has set out for him.

Having read the teaching of Krishna, we have a choice. We can continue with our lives as we have always lived them or we can go the way of Uddhava ~ into the still mountains of the Self. If we follow Uddhava's path we may well continue with the lives we lead now but our entire inner orientation will have changed. We will view this world from the vantage point of the mountain top, never again falling into the trap of false identification, which leads to sorrow upon sorrow.

If we light a lamp of devotion to illuminate the path of our lives, if we live in the spirit of renunciation ~ not seeking our own good but seeking always the Source ~ we will light a lamp for all.

1 The devotee Uddhava said,

This practice of Yoga is extremely difficult
For one who has not yet
Mastered the senses or the mind.
Surely there is an easier way
To attain this realization.

2 O Lotus-eyed Beloved,
Sovereign of all creation,
I know that often
Those engaged in these Yogic practices
Become frustrated:
Unable to still the mind,
They do not reach a meditative state
And become despondent.

3 For this reason
Those that can discern
The real from the unreal
Take refuge in your lotus-feet,

Which shower all with bliss.
Those who do not know this,
And who take pride
In their accomplishments as Yogis,
Are defeated by your all-powerful maya.

4 O Infallible One,
Befriender of all,
While gods like Brahma
Place their crown upon your footstool,
You deal lovingly with everyone
Who comes to you.
You shower with blessings
Even the servants and animals
Who seek your company.
For when you incarnated as Prince Rama,
You befriended and gave affection
To the monkey, Hanuman.

5 Anyone who knows
The grace that you bestow
On those who come to you with devotion
Would turn away from the path
That does not lead to you.
You are the Beloved,
The Self of the entire universe,
The giver of all wishes.
Who could reject the grace you bestow?
Who could possibly forget you
And embrace the world instead,
Knowing that such an embrace
Would end in forgetting you?
There is absolutely nothing that those of us
Who are engaged in service
In the dust of your feet
Lack, need or want.

6 O you that are the All-in-All,
Neither poets nor Yogic adepts,
Though they were to be given a lifetime

Equal to that of the god Brahma,
Could express their gratitude and debt to you.
You reveal yourself by removing our ignorance
And you do this in a dual form ~
As the teacher who stands without,
And as the Self within.

7 Blessed Shuka said,

Thus being asked by Uddhava,
Whose affection was sincere,
Radiant Krishna, the Supreme,
The One who is also the three ~
Brahma, Vishnu and Shiva ~
Smiled his brilliant smile
And proceeded to answer.

8 The Radiant One, Krishna, said,

Yes, let me tell you
Some spiritual practices
That will lead to me,
And through which ~
When they are practiced with
Faith and devotion to me ~
You will overcome death.

9 Place your mind
And all that it contains
In me.
Offer it all to me.
Do the work calmly
That is associated with your earthly duties
And offer it all to me.

10 Take shelter from this world
In sacred places
Where those devoted to me reside.
Imitate the conduct of those
Who are devoted to me.
You will find them everywhere ~
Among gods, people and demons.

11 Individually or with others
On ekadashi[1] and other sacred days,
Organize gatherings and festivals
Where people can sing and dance to my glory
Even as they would before a king in splendor.

12 With a pure heart
Resting in a pure mind,
See only me
As the immortal Self
In all beings.
See this Self as that
Which is internal to you
And external to you ~
As expansive as the sky.

13 Enlightened Uddhava,
One who gazes upon the world
From this vantage point,
And sees in all living beings
My presence,
Giving respect and consideration
To all that they encounter,

14 Who looks with an equal eye
Upon both the high-born and the low-born,
The spark and the blazing sun,
The tenderhearted and the cruel,
Is considered by me to be a sage.

15 One who is always
Present to my Presence in all,
Quickly overcomes any tendencies towards
Rivalry, envy and conceit,
Which are born of the idea-of-"I."

16 Disregarding the contempt and ridicule
Of friends and acquaintances,
And casting aside embarrassment
With awareness of the body

Prostrate sincerely before all:
Be they outcasts, dogs, asses or cows.

17 Worship everyone in this way
In thought, word and deed ~
And my Presence within all
Will soon be revealed.

18 That vision, in which the Truth is revealed
And Brahman is seen to exist everywhere,
Will liberate you from all doubts
And all effortful striving.

19 This form of worship
Is the highest:
With body, mind and speech
Regard all beings as myself.

20 My dear Uddhava,
I have established devotion
As a spiritual pathway
By which the ultimate truth may be known.
None who walk it will suffer from want.

21 Uddhava, most pious of men,
Whatever worldly activity ~
Even if it is weeping through fear ~
Is offered to me
Without desire for reward,
Is the most exalted spiritual path
That anyone can walk.

22 This teaching is indeed
The wisdom of the wise
And the intelligence of the discerning:
Through it one uses the unreal
To achieve the real.

23 I have now taught you
The knowledge of the Absolute
In general and in its particulars.

Even for the gods,
This teaching is difficult to grasp.

24 I have given you this teaching
In a clear and reasoned way,
Just as I have given it before.
Anyone who understands it
Will be freed from doubts
And attain liberation.

25 Anyone who treasures in their mind
This dialogue between us,
In which my teaching is imparted,
Will realize the immortal and everlasting
Brahman that lies in hidden in the Vedas.

26 To one who passes on this teaching,
Which bestows on my devotees
The highest knowledge,
To that one
I give myself completely.

27 Whoever daily reads aloud
This sacred and purifying teaching ~
Thereby lighting a lamp
With which others may see ~
I will purify.

28 Anyone who listens daily
To this teaching
With attentive devotion
Will never become bound
To the activities of this world,
Even while engaged in them.

29 My dear friend Uddhava,
Has the true nature of Brahman
Now been understood by you?
And have the illusion and sadness
Now been lifted from your mind?

30 Do not pass on these teachings
To anyone who is arrogant,
Without faith or deceitful,
Unwilling to listen
Or lacking in devotion.

31 You should tell only them
To those who are free
From these weaknesses
And who are devoted
And dedicated to the welfare of the saintly.
When devotees are present
Who are not of caste
Or are women,
They too may listen to these teachings.

32 The seeker needs no further knowledge
Than the knowledge imparted in this teaching ~
Just as nothing remains to be drunk
After drinking the nectar of immortality.

33 For all devotees
Who are like you, O Uddhava,
I embody all that may be gained
Through the pursuit of
Religious merit
And the performance of duty,
The practice of Yoga,
The business of agriculture
And even through the wielding of power.

34 Those who surrender
All that they do
And all that they are
Shall receive my grace
And become fit for that Self-realization
Whereby they become One with me.

35 Blessed Shuka resumed,

Having been given this teaching
Of the direct and excellent path of Yoga

By Shri Krishna himself,
Uddhava stood in silence
Unable to utter even a word.
His palms were joined
And his heart overflowing
As tears rolled down his cheeks.

36 Taking control of himself,
And knowing how truly blessed he had been,
He bowed down and
Touched with his head
The lotus-feet of the Prince of the Yadhavas.
Then he spoke these words.

37 The devotee Uddhava said,

O Creator of Brahma,
The thick darkness of ignorance
That I have held on to for all this time
Has been dispelled by your words.
Can fear of the dark and the cold
Prevail against one who has found
The light and warmth of fire?

38 The light of wisdom,
Which your power of maya veiled,
Has been restored to me, your servant,
Through your own compassion.
How could anyone
Conscious of this compassion
Forsake your feet
And seek refuge elsewhere?

39 The ropes of affection,
Which bound me to family and friends,
Ties whose real nature
I could not perceive
Through the veil of maya,
You have cut asunder
With the sword of knowledge.

40 All praises are due to you,
O Great Master of all Yoga,
In you alone I take refuge.
Tell me this one last time,
How I may remain forever faithful
To your lotus-feet alone.

41 The Radiant One, Krishna, replied,

Go now, O Uddhava,
Directly to the hermitage of Badarika,[2]
Which is my sacred place.
Purify yourself there
By bathing in the cleansing waters
That flow from my feet.

42 Gaze upon the great Alakananda river[3]
And be cleansed by that gaze.
Wearing only the bark of trees
And eating only their fruits, nuts and berries,
Be happy and free from all desires.

43 Tolerant of all the pairs of opposites
And with a saintly demeanor,
Live your life peacefully
In the knowledge
I have imparted to you,
Which controls the senses
And fixes the mind
On the goal of Self-realization.

44 Let all your actions and all your thoughts
Be centered on me and me alone.
Engage yourself in such actions
That will be pleasing to me.
In this manner you will transcend
The three destinies that nature offers,
Celestial, human or animal ~
Which are dictated by the three gunas ~
And you will instead merge with me.

⁴⁵ Blessed Shuka resumed,

Instructed thus by Shri Krishna,
Uddhava, with his palms joined,
Walked around the Radiant One,
Keeping him on his right.
Then he again placed his head
On Krishna's feet
And bathed them with his tears
Brought on by the thought
Of being separated
From this gracious Beloved.

⁴⁶ With his heart breaking
At the thought of this separation,
Uddhava accepted from Krishna
The gift of his own wooden sandals,
And placing them on his head
He departed.

⁴⁷ Having firmly placed the Radiant One in his heart,
Uddhava went directly to Badarika as instructed.
There he lived according to these teachings
And attained that blessed state of oneness
With Shri Hari, the Radiant One.

⁴⁸ This sweet teaching
Contains an ocean of bliss
Given to the devotee Uddhava
By Shri Krishna,
Whose feet the masters of Yoga worship.
Anyone who partakes of it
With genuine faith
Is assured of liberation.

⁴⁹ I prostrate before the Supreme One,
Shri Krishna, source of the Vedas.
As a bee draws the essence from the flower,
His teaching has given us the essence of the Vedas.
Through his mercy his devotees have drunk nectar
From the ocean of bliss.

❄ Afterword

Uddhava has taken up his mission. He has accepted the dharma given to him by his guru, Krishna, and attained the experience of Oneness. But what of Bhagavan Shri Krishna, the complete avatar, the teacher and friend of all, the Radiant One?

In the subsequent pages of the *Bhagavatha Purana*, Sage Shuka describes what happens next. Knowing that Dvaraka will be destroyed, Krishna sends the women, children and older men to safety in Sankhoddara. The younger men are asked to go to Prabhasa to purify themselves. But the cleansing is to no avail and the destiny of the Yadus is fulfilled when they attack Krishna, and he and Balarama finally destroy them. After this battle, while he rests beside a tree, Krishna is pierced in the foot by the arrow of a hunter. This too is as it has been foretold, and, in a final moment of meditation, Krishna leaves this earthly plane.

Did Krishna Vasudeva die? The verses of the *Bhagavatha Purana* that relate to this question are compelling and mysterious:

> *With Brahma, the celestial sages and the gods before him,*
> *All of whom he knew were none other than himself,*
> *The Radiant One, Krishna, closed his lotus-eyes,*
> *And withdrew himself into the Self.*
>
> *By practicing the Yogic method of Agni dharana,*
> *He burnt the body which had delighted all who knew it*
> *And which, when meditated on,*
> *Grants grace to the devotee.*
> *Then he entered his own realm.*
>
> (Book 2, 31:5–6)

The word that is mysterious here is dagdhva. Some translators have read the text as "adagdhva," "without burning," and others, like Swami Venkatesananda, have read it as "dagdhva," "with burning." A final clue is in Verse 13 of the same dialogue:

The Radiant One, Shri Krishna,
Had the power to create, sustain and destroy
All of creation.
Yet he did not wish
To preserve his body here any longer
Even though he could.
For he had always taught that the perishable
Is not worth saving.

Did the body of Shri Krishna die? That is for each devotee to decide for him or herself ~ the texts leave enough ambiguity for us to answer in the way that each finds most acceptable.

Perhaps Krishna dies every time we do not let him live through our lives in the manner he prescribed. Perhaps Krishna lives in us when we open our hearts to his teachings and purify ourselves in the ways he taught ~ through love and compassion to all beings, exercised in the spirit of renunciation. Thus, when Uddhava asks, "Take me with you," Krishna answers through the entire *Uddhava Gita* by telling him how to follow the path to that which he seeks. When we follow that path, surely Krishna lives and Vaikuntha becomes the space of own hearts, as Dvaraka ~ the idea-of-"I" ~ is submerged.

Ram Tirtha, the twentieth-century saint and mystic, echoed this teaching when he said: "When you seek me do not search at the circumference where nothing meets ~ go to the center where all things meet."

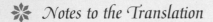 *Notes to the Translation*

Introduction

1. Bhattacharya, B., *Saivism and the Phallic World*, Volume 1, Oxford and IBH Publishing Co., New Delhi, 1975, page 46.

Dialogue 1

1. Brahma is the creator of the Universe. He is part of the Hindu trinity (trimurthi) consisting of Brahma, Vishnu the preserver, who descends into the world of matter as an avatar, and Shiva the destroyer.

2. The word Bhagavan is translated throughout as "the Radiant One." Of all the incarnations of Vishnu, Krishna alone is a total incarnation (purnavatara). The embodiment of love and compassion, he teaches the path of bhakti, or devotion. The name Krishna means "the dark one," which suggests to some historians that he was dark in color and therefore belonged to a people of a non-Aryan tradition that was later incorporated into the Aryan pantheon. His name could also relate to the dark age (the Kali Yuga) that comes with his death. In the *Bhagavatham*, Krishna is the supreme One.

3. The text actually reads "Brahmatma jaih," or "Brahma and his sons." Sanaka and his brothers are the first born. Although not mentioned in the text by name, Sanaka's presence is implied.

4. Verses 2 and 3 enumerate the celestial beings that descend to Dvaraka. Indra is generally taken to be the king of the gods and ruler of heaven. The Maruts, a term usually applied to the forty-nine wind gods, divinities of the sphere between heaven and earth, are said to represent the life-breath. The Aditiyas, sons of the goddess Aditi (the vast primordial space of creation), are embodiments of the law by which all social relations are governed. The Vasus, described in the *Rig Veda* as the attendants of Indra, are the Pole Star (Dhruva), Water (Apa), Moon (Soma), Earth (Dhara), Wind (Anila), Fire (Anala), Dawn (Prabhasa), Light (Pratyusa). The word Vasu can mean "that which surrounds" and in Shri Sankaracharya's commentary on the *Chandogya Upanishad,* the Vasus are so named because "they dwell or cause to dwell." Thus they are the spheres of existence. The Ashvins are the twin deities of good fortune and health, also considered the physicians of the gods. The Rbhus were originally mortals and attained the status of gods by performing religious rites with expert skill. Angiras, the god of magic lore or, according to the *Mahabharata*, a rishi, is one of the cosmic principles. The Rudras, the first creation of Rudra, belong to the second stage of cosmic evolution, when the life-principle first appears. The Vishvedevas are the universal principles. In *The Myths and Gods of India* (Inner Traditions, Vermont, 1991, page 255) Alain Danielou quotes from the Devisukta of the *Rig Veda:* "I wander with the principles of life (Rudras), with the spheres-of-existence (Vasus), with the sovereign principles (Aditiyas) and the all-pervading gods (Vishvedevas)." The Sadyas are the deities that govern the means of realization. The Gandharvas are the celestial musicians. The Apsaras are the celestial dancers but also the unmanifest essence of things occurring in nature, like water. I think of the Apsaras as unmanifest potential. The Nagas are serpents. The Siddhas are beings who have attained perfection, and the Caranas are their admiring retinue. The Guhyaka are a class of demigods who, along with the Yakshas, are attendants of Kubera and guardians of his treasure. The Guhyaka (meaning "those reared in a secret place") are so named because they are said to have been raised in mountain caves. The Rishis are the ancient saints and sages who were the seers of the Vedic hymns. The Pitara are the departed forefathers or ancestors. The Vidyadharas are the ancient bearers of wisdom who are able to change their form at will. The Kinnaras are celestial humans who have the head of a horse; also attached to Kubera they sing the praises of the gods.

5. The Vedas are the primary scriptures of Hinduism. They are considered to contain the sum of all knowledge, "seen" in its entirety by the ancient rishis and hence regarded as the word of divine revelation. The word veda comes from vid, "to know." The Vedas are said to have been put into their present form by the sage Veda Vyasa. They were first written down (in Sanskrit) thousands of years BCE, although they existed long before that. Four Vedas survive: the *Rig Veda*, the *Yajur Veda*, the *Sama Veda* and the *Atharva Veda*.

6. Krishna is greeted here as the Prince of the Yadus. He was an incarnation of Vishnu who descended from his heavenly realm of Vaikuntha and was born into the Yadu dynasty, a warlike clan situated in Dvaraka. (Present-day Dvaraka is on the north-west coast of India.) The incarnation of Krishna was to "relieve the earth of the burden of evil" and by the end of the *Bhagavatham* he has fulfilled this destiny by passing supremacy among clans to the Pandavas and overseeing the destruction of the Yadu dynasty.

7. One of the most prominent myths associated with Vishnu is the story of the three steps, which is based on a creation myth that stems from the Vedic concept of measuring, spreading out and holding up all the parts of the universe. One of Vishnu's incarnations was as the dwarf Vamana. The story goes that a king called Bali earned rulership of the three worlds (heaven, earth and the space in between) through his good deeds. The gods implored Vishnu to restore Indra to his sovereignty and Vishnu obliged by appearing before Bali as the dwarf Vamana. He asked for a wish to be granted and Bali agreed, whereupon Vamana said that he wanted as much of the kingdom as could be covered by three of his strides. Bali readily agreed and when Vishnu, with just two strides, had already covered heaven and earth Bali offered his head for the third stride. Vamana let Bali keep the netherworlds.

8. The words appearing here as "matter" and "spirit" are "Prakriti" and "Purusha" in the text. These are two terms that come from the Samkhya philosophy, which is generally interpreted as a dualist system in which matter and spirit are seen as separate. However, B. Bhattacharya points out that these terms have a more ancient tradition, relating back to Tantra, in which they mean "nature" (Prakriti) and "witness consciousness" (Purusha). "The Prakriti of Samkhya is but a subtlety of the formed body; nothing individually different from Purusha." The manifest individual can be said to be Prakriti, the outcome of ignorance and unknowing, which are themselves illusory. The two are only as separate as "... food and taste or light and sight" (Bhattacharya, page 211). For the mystic, all forms of matter ultimately lead back to consciousness.

Dialogue 2

1. Krishna incarnated with his brother, Balarama.

2. Having accomplished the goal of ridding the earth of the burden of evil, Krishna knew it was time to return to the heavenly realm of Vaikuntha. He observed that the clan he had been born into had become successful and arrogant. As always, Krishna allows the evolution of his will through the action of others. When Yadu youths insult the sages and invoke a curse of destruction, Krishna mitigates the curse but does not completely nullify it. The Yadus fulfill their own destiny and are finally destroyed.

3. The cosmology of the Puranas is highly detailed. At the end of every kalpa (eon), the universe is destroyed by a conflagration. It is then submerged, in embryonic form, in the cosmic waters, while Brahma has a well-earned sleep. When a new kalpa is to be created, Brahma is awakened. Each kalpa consists of four yugas. They begin with the best, when creation is closest to its divine origin, and end with the worst, the Kali Yuga, when the divine is most hidden and spiritual life is at its lowest. It is said that we are now in the Kali Yuga that began with the death of Krishna. It will end with the coming of the incarnation of Vishnu known as Kalki.

4. Narayana is one of the twenty-two names of Vishnu. While the universe lies dormant in the cosmic ocean, Vishnu sleeps floating on the serpent, Sesa. He is then called Narayana ("moving on the waters"). Narayana can also mean "the abode of humankind." The image conveyed in this verse is of a sage experiencing himself as silent and immeasurable as Narayana resting on the cosmic water.

5. Samkhya and Yoga are usually studied together. Both these orthodox Hindu systems can lay claim to being even more ancient than the Vedas. Samkhya is often described as an atheistic system but, while analytical, its subject is transcendence. Samkhya's legendary founder was the ancient sage Kapila. It teaches the existence of the tattvas, the twenty-five basic constituents of matter drawn from Prakriti (usually translated as "creation" but is just as appropriately "evolution"). From Prakriti, buddhi evolves, an intelligent awareness that in the *Bhagavatham* is "Mahat Tattva," or "Cosmic Intelligence." From buddhi arises the ahamkara, or idea-of-"I." Next to evolve is matter in its most subtle form, called the tanmatras: smell, taste, form, touch, sound. From the tanmatras evolve the mahabhutas: space, air, fire, water and earth. From these evolve the jnanendriya, the five means of knowledge: hearing, touch, sight, taste and smell. From these evolve the karmendriya, the five means of action: speech, movement of the hands, walking or movement of the feet, evacuation and procreation. Finally manas, or mind, evolves, which mediates between buddhi and the jnanendriyas and karmendriyas. The twenty-fifth constituent is Purusha. Samkhya was an early attempt by humankind to find an answer to the riddle of life through an examination and enumeration of its parts. The word Samkhya means "the count."

Yoga (particularly Ashtanga Yoga: see note 1, Dialogue 14) is very closely related to Samkhya. Yoga is a system of self-analysis and self-discipline. It seeks a state of higher understanding through control of the body, senses and mind. Yoga brings one more component to its analysis: Ishvara, which to the Yogi comprises both Prakriti and Purusha. The word Yoga, an active verb that comes from the root *yuj* ("join") implies movement. Thus Yoga recognizes that we are fragmented, not whole, and that a joining, a making whole, is necessary. In the course of its long history, Yoga has also come to be used as a noun, indicating one of the six accepted systems of philosophy within Hinduism.

The *Uddhava Gita*, the *Bhagavad Gita* and the *Svetasvathara Upanishad* can all be seen as texts which seek to synthesize the Yoga and Samkhya systems. The difference between Yoga and Samkhya, on the one hand, and Vedanta, on the other, is not great. Samkhya does not disavow the popular bhakti movement of devotion for the One through the many. Yoga positively encourages it, through the use of the ishta devata (see note 3 to Dialogue 9). In Vedanta, the many forms are gathered together into the single One as Om or Brahman.

Dialogue 4

1. "The undifferentiated One without a second" refers to the state in which one cannot differentiate between consciousness and matter. It is the state between creative cycles when what is, is.

Dialogue 5

1. The word used to denote duties is sva-dharma. The English "duty" does the word "dharma" no justice at all. Literally, it means "that which is established or firm": a statute, a law or a prescribed conduct. "Sva-dharma" means one's own duty. Hindus refer to their religion as the "Sanatana Dharma" ~ the "Eternal Law." To confine the word to "duty" or "law" is to bind it to a limited understanding. Dharma is revealed in the Vedas. It is "truth" or "ethics"; it is also that by which the universe is upheld and which makes each thing what it is and not something else. It is religion and philosophical reasoning bound with action and practice. The ultimate dharma is to know Brahman, through the practice of dharma.

2. In this experience of the Ultimate, all duality ends and the knower and the known merge into Brahman. Subject experiencing object no longer exists ~ the fire loses its fuel.

3. The next few verses appear to be a refutation of the Mimamsa view. Two main schools of thought developed from the Vedas. One is Purva Mimamsa, or simply Mimamsa, and the other is Uttara Mimamsa, or, most commonly, Vedanta. Mimamsa focuses on the correct performance of Vedic rituals. In effect, it is both a manual and a mandate for priests, who are in the fortunate position of being the main interpreters of the Vedas and the only performers of Vedic ritual. Because the results of any ritual are dependent on not only correct performance but also on those performing, lower castes, women and disabled people were not permitted to attend. In the Mimamsa view, performance of the sacrifice leads to apurva, or "that which was not before." In other words, what did not exist before could be produced by performing a ritual.

Vedanta means literally "the end of the Vedas," referring to the Upanishads, the last part and "inner teaching" of the Vedas. In contrast to Mimamsa, which looks for salvation through ritual, Vedanta seeks salvation through the process of introspection and analysis culminating in subjective experience. In its primary text, the *Purva Mimasaka Sutra*, Mimamsa accepts the reality of the multiplicity of forms and rejects the primacy of consciousness. In contrast, Vedanta seeks the experience of the oneness of Brahman. Vedanta is by far the most prevalent and important school of thought in Hinduism.

Dialogue 6

1. This verse expresses the advaitist (non-dualist) view that only the One exists. This view raises the question of why, if Brahman is pure and perfect, is the world impure and imperfect? If imperfection is produced by an agency other than Brahman, then Brahman itself cannot be free. It was the great sage and mystic, Shankaracharya, who answered this question with a paradox. He said that the world was created, evolved and exists ~ but he also said that the world does not exist. It all depends on your point of view. If you identify with the ahamkara, the-idea-of-"I," you see a world of good and bad, pain and pleasure, in which multiple entities live and die ~ an illusion superimposed on to reality. However, through "enlightenment" another view can be seen, in which only Brahman is. The attainment of this view is the advaitic definition of salvation and it is reached by the means of knowledge and meditation.

Advaita has become the most widely accepted of the three Indian schools of theological interpretation. The second school is the vishishtadvaitist (qualified non-dualist) view that the one Reality and "the many" are real but not the same, although existing in close contact with each other. The third school is dvaita (dualism). The dualist view is that there is a real and irreconcilable distinction between the individual and the Absolute. These different views all evolved from the Vedic traditions. All three schools interpret both the *Bhagavad Gita* and *Uddhava Gita* to support their own position.

2. This verse is a reference to the Vedantist versus Mimamsakas debate.

3. Up to this moment, Krishna has been advocating the path of jnana (knowledge) as the means to Self-realization. He now begins to outline the path of bhakti (adoration or devotion). The message of bhakti, elaborated throughout this text, is central to the teaching of Krishna. In bhakti, inner purity, devotion and faith take absolute precedence over social status. This devotion is far more important than scriptural injunctions or ritual. In fact, ritual is made potent only by the devotion of the participant. Krishna is advocating not the rejection of knowledge but the involvement of the whole person ~ body, mind (including the emotions) and spirit. Against the quest for the perfect ritual, performed in a narrowly prescribed manner by a chosen elite, comes this glorious emergence of spiritual devotion. Many scholars and religions reject bhakti as unscientific and primitive. This

perhaps indicates the harboring of a vanity. The question is not whether emotion is present, but where it is being directed.

4. A mandala is a geometric shap or apattern that is often "perceived" in meditation and which usually signifies an aspect of the infinite.

5. A mantra is a mystical word or sound, Vedic or Tantric in origin, that is chanted or repeated mentally during meditation as a point of focus. The mantra is usually imparted to the initiate by the guru.

Dialogue 7

1. The long tradition of sannyasa ("putting down," "laying aside," "abandoning") survives to this day. In Hinduism there are four distinct phases of life. Brahmacharya is student life, from birth to the age of twenty-five. Grihastha is married life and the raising of children, from about twenty-five to fifty. Vanapratha is retirement to a quiet place, once family financial affairs have been handed over to the children, usually from fifty to seventy-five. And sannyasa is renunciation, at seventy-five. However, many sannyasins in India have skipped phases two and three.

2. Prahlada was the son of King Hiranyakasipu, who claimed rulership of the world. When Prahlada declared that Vishnu was sovereign, his father tried to kill him, but repeatedly failed due to Vishnu's intervention. Finally Vishnu took the form of a lion-man, Narasimha, and killed Hiranyakasipu.

3. Vibhasana was the virtuous younger brother of Ravana, the demonic opponent of Rama in the *Ramayana*. Sugriva was the monkey king whose armies, under Hanuman, assisted Rama in defeating Ravana. Jambavan (meaning "jaws" or "eye-tooth") was a demon killed by Vishnu. Gajendra was a king changed into an elephant by his own curse. Attacked by a crocodile while bathing in a river, Gajendra prayed to Vishnu, who helped him to free himself. His name became synonymous with faith. Krishna goes on to name a number of figures from Hindu mythology whose lives were transformed by associating with saints, sages and devotees.

4. Anyone who has attended a Yoga class in the West will be familiar with the word prana. It originates from "pri," meaning "to fill." Prana is the power by which matter is established and organized through the tattvas and under the governance of the gunas. Where I have not used the Sanskrit word itself, I have translated it as "vitality."

5. Yoga postulates the existence of an inner or "subtle" body that roughly corresponds to the physical body, but is the field of prana rather than blood, nerves and chemicals. Prana flows along nadi, or meridians. Chief among these is the sushumna, which corresponds to the spine. It begins at the perineum and culminates at the crown of the head. Lying dormant at the base of the sushumna nadi is Kundalini Shakti. This is a primal power awaiting awakening through the mystical practices of Yoga. Once awakened, Kundalini rises up the sushumna to the crown of the head, where it is united with Ishvara. It is this moment of union that constitutes samadhi, or enlightenment. Along the sushumna are the chakras, the "spinning wheels." Prana enters the crown of the head, flows down the sushumna and into the subtle body via the chakras. Each chakra corresponds to one of the tattvas and gives a certain characteristic to the prana, which, in turn, animates the physical body. Kundalini rests in the muladhara chakra, which corresponds to the earth tattva. The chakra at the heart, anahata, holds the air tattva, with its corresponding sound, tanmatra. Anahata literally means "sound without striking." Silence is broken by the agitation of the gunas as it is wounded with nad, the primordial sound.

6. The cycle of birth, death and rebirth.

Dialogue 8

1. This verse is a beautiful reflection of two verses in the *Bhagavad Gita*:

> *When a man thinks of an object*
> *Attachment for that object arises ~*
> *From attachment desire is born*
> *And from desire anger arises.*
>
> *From anger will come delusion*
> *From delusion loss of integrity*
> *From loss of integrity comes*
> *Destruction of discrimination*
> *Then all is lost.*
>
> (2:62–3)

2. The auspicious hours for meditation ~ dawn, noon and dusk ~ are called the brahmamahurta.

3. Keshava is one of the names of Krishna and means "the one with long hair."

4. The divine swan, Hamsa, is said to be able to draw up the milk and leave the water when the two are mixed together. Paramahamsa, "great swan," is the traditional manner of addressing one who has attained the ability to discriminate real from unreal.

5. The words Atman and Jiva are usually translated as "soul." However, while "soul" in a Western context is separate from God, there is no difference between Atman, Jiva and Brahman. All are the same thing ~ the eternal Presence that is located nowhere in particular but everywhere at once. Generally speaking, that Presence is referred to as "Atman" when speaking of it directly, without embodiment, and as "Jiva" when speaking of it as that which animates the individual with consciousness. That same Presence is "Brahman" when referring to its transcendent reality.

Dialogue 9

1. Shankarshana is a reference to Krishna's brother, Balarama, who because he changed wombs is called "drawn out." This points to the fact that Balarama and Krishna are one.

2. In the meditation practice that follows, Krishna recommends the use of the ishta devata. The practice comes under the auspices of bhakti, where an image of the chosen deity is adopted as the point of focus, along with the mantra used in meditation. The ishta devata is the intimate, personal form through which the bhakta chooses to relate to the impersonal, formless Brahman. The ishta devata is not an antithesis of Brahman as the One, the all-pervading being. It is a means of access to that One. An intense relationship is created with the ishta devata that has a reality only in the inner being of the devotee who, at the moment of meditation, sees the image dissolve into all things and into that which transcends all things. The purpose of the ishta devata is not as a model for others to follow but as a single focus in which the devotee can become entirely lost.

Dialogue 11

1. This dialogue between Krishna and Arjuna takes place in the *Bhagavad Gita*.

2. Hiranyagarbah is the designation of the Absolute as the Golden Embryo, the germinal matter in which the universe is a potentiality.

3. The Sanskrit alphabet has fifteen vowels in all, beginning with A (pronounced as in "father").

4. The three-lined Gayatri mantra is the most famous of the Vedic mantras. Most brahmin and kshatriya boys are taught it as part of the initiation process they undergo at puberty.

5. In Hindu mythology, Agni is the god of fire and the first priest.

6. Bhrigu was one of the seven great sages, son of Manu (the progenitor of the human race) and father of the sage Shukra. Narada was one of the sons of Brahma, a messenger between gods and men, and a great sage. Kamadhenu is a wish-fulfilling cow associated with time.

7. Sage Kapila was the founder of Samkhya. Half-vulture and half-man, Garuda is Vishnu's chosen vehicle (each god has an animal as his or her vehicle and symbol). Daksha is one of the sons of Brahma, whose daughter, Uma, married Shiva. Aryama is the god of custom, a son of Aditi and therefore one of the Adityas. He is also the counterpart of Daksha: in this world, Daksha stands for ritual skill; in heaven, Daksha is Aryaman, the embodiment of honor and chivalry.

8. Airavata is a white elephant, the vehicle of Indra.

9. Yama is the god of death.

10. Mount Meru is a sacred mountain in the Himalayan range that appears repeatedly in Hindu mythology.

11. Vashishta is one of the foremost sages in Hindu mythology. He taught Rama, the first human incarnation of Vishnu. Brihaspati is sometimes a god and sometimes a rishi, son of Angiras. Kartikaya is a son of Shiva and a formidable general and strategist.

12. Satarupa ("one with a hundred forms") was the first woman; the daughter of Brahma and the wife or mother of Manu. Svayambhu is the self out of which the First One, Svayambhuva, evolved. Sanatkumara is the most prominent of the four mind-born sons of Brahma.

13. Margashirsha is mid-November to mid-December. Abhijit is the last constellation of Sravanna in jyotish (Vedic) astrology.

14. Vasudeva is the father of Krishna, a son of Shura in the Yadu clan.

15. Kusha (poa cynosuroides) is a sacred grass with long pointed stalks used in religious ceremonies.

Dialogue 12

1. In Hindu society, the conduct and duties (dharma) which relate directly to one's caste (varna) and one's stage of life (ashrama) are of utmost importance. They are known collectively as the varnashrama dharma.

2. There are two Madhus mentioned in the *Bhagavatham*. One is the demon of this verse, the other is an ancestor of Krishna.

3. In the varnashrama system, a young boy would enter the home of his guru at around puberty, to learn the scriptures, ethics and practical skills. Many young brahmacharins would live in the guru's dwelling, called a gurukul.

4. A mala can be a garland of flowers, placed around the neck of the deity, or a string of prayer beads used to recite mantras or the names of gods. Usually it will have 108 beads made of wood or stone. Worshipers of Vishnu often use a tulsi mala made of the wood of the sacred basil tree, while worshipers of Shiva will use a rudraksha mala, made of dried berries of the "red-eyed bush."

Dialogue 13

1. These austerities are known as tapas, or "heat." Tapas, in its traditional sense, means subjecting the body to physical stress (such as surrounding oneself by fires in the heat of the midday sun) to induce an awareness that is beyond the body.

2. Agnihotra, or havan, is a fire ceremony where oblations are offered to Agni. Performed by the initiated at specified times using special mantras, it is one of the most ancient ceremonies in existence.

3. This verse alludes to the havan ritual that takes place when one enters the sannyasa stage of life. The initiates ceremonially offer themselves and their past relationships into the fire. After being taken through the funeral rite by a priest, they are born again as one who has died to the past.

4. The sannyasin renounces heaven, earth and the space in-between as part of the initiation ceremony, showing a loss of ambition for anything that may be gained from these.

Dialogue 14

1. The tradition laid down by Patanjali is Ashtanga Yoga ~ the "eight-limbed" Yoga that moves us from the illusion of individual identity to the realization of a cosmic identity beyond the limits of time and space. These ashtanga, or limbs, are: yama (discipline related to dealings with others) and niyama (self-discipline); asana (bodily discipline based on posture); pranayama (control of the prana); pratiharya (withdrawal of the senses); dharana (fixing the mind); dhyana (meditation); samadhi (liberation). These "limbs" are yoked through bhakti (devotion), jnana (knowledge) and karma (action). There are two kinds of jnana: bauddha (intellectual) and paurusa (intuitive). The most conducive to liberation is the latter, which the Yogi seeks to develop through various practices.

Dialogue 16

1. This verse seems to establish Bhagavan Shri Krishna as an ecologist.

2. Ghee is unsalted butter that has gone through a clarification process.

3. "Subtle as a lotus stalk" could be a reference to the sushumna nadi.

4. One of India's greatest gifts to the world was the Sanskrit alphabet, the remote mother of all Indo-European languages. Unlike the haphazard Roman alphabet, which grew more organically, Sanskrit is systematically ordered. It was the first language to develop within the framework of rules recorded by one Panini in the 4th century BCE.

Dialogue 17

1. Uddhava is again referring to the different schools of thought regarding the tattvas.

Dialogue 18

1. Avanti is now Malwa.

2. King Khatvanga was granted the knowledge of his imminent death and was able to obtain Self-realization in his remaining moments.

Dialogue 19

Davies, P., and J. Gribbin, *The Matter Myth*, Viking, UK, 1991, page 302.

Dialogue 21

1. This story first appears in the *Rig Veda*. Pururavas was the grandson of Manu, and a powerful king in his own right. When Urvashi left him, Pururavas was completely distraught but eventually regained his composure, and he and Urvashi were reunited. Their names are invoked during the sacred fire ceremony where they become the upper and lower kindling sticks. The ghee is called by the name of their child, Ayu.

Dialogue 22

1. The Narada referred to here is the sage who was the author of the *Narada Bhakti Sutras*.

2. "Tantra arose as the sum total of man's knowledge of the objective world around him. It was a way of life that sought the significance of knowledge, not in the realization of an illusory absolute, but in the day-to-day activities of men, in the simple facts of life like agriculture, cattle-breeding, distillation,

iron-smelting, etc., and in experimental sciences like alchemy, medicine, embryology, physiology and so forth, with a deliberate theoretical orientation that the structures of the microcosm and the macrocosm are identical and that the key to the knowledge of nature is to be found in the body." (Bhattacharyya, N.N., *History of the Tantric Religion*, Manohar, New Delhi, 1992, page 1).

3. The practice of purifying one's self, the place, the mantra, the articles of worship and even the deity date back to Tantric practices called pancasuddhi.

4. This relates to the story in which the gods and demons churn the milky ocean and many things issue forth, including the famous Kaustubha gem.

5. The mark on Krishna or Vishnu's chest symbolizing the eternal presence of Shri (the female deity within the male).

6. Vishvakshena is the chief attendant of Vishnu.

7. The first hymn mentioned, the "Svarna-gharma" (beginning with the words "Survarnam gharmam parivedavenam) is lost to us. The second is the "Mahapurusa Vidya," which is the first verse of the *Vishnu Purana*. Most scholars agree that the "Rajana" and "Rohina Samas" are lost, although we know that one line of the "Rajana" begins, "Indram naro nemadhita."

8. A mark made on the forehead between the eyebrows.

9. Traditionally the image is bathed in milk, yoghurt, ghee, honey and sugar.

10. The Purusha Shuktam can be found in its entirety in the *Rig Veda* and the *Yajur Veda*.

11. Ritualized acts of worship which cleanse and transform are known as Kriya Yoga.

Dialogue 23

1. Laszlo, E., *The Whispering Pond*, Element, London, 1996, page 28.

Dialogue 24

1. The eleventh day after the full moon.

2. Badarika is present-day Badirinath ~ still a place of pilgrimage for people from around the globe. High in the Himalayas, it is only accessible in the summer months. When the priests leave in autumn to travel back down to the south of India, they light an oil lamp that burns steadily under the snows until the spring thaw, when the temple doors are again opened. An ancient image of Krishna is installed there.

3. The Alakananda river and the Bagirathi river join to form the Ganges. The confluence of these two rivers is considered an auspicious place to bathe.

❀ Sanskrit Glossary

adharma absence of righteousness.

advaita (a "not," dva "two") non-dualism; the teaching that declares all existence is one. A philosophical system of Hinduism.

agni fire.

ahamkara (aham "I," kara "maker") the idea-of-"I"; the ego; that which separates us from others; an evolution of Prakriti.

ahimsa non-violence.

ajnanan absence of knowledge.

akasha space.

anahata (an "not," hata "struck") mystical sound produced without striking; the anahata chakra is the seat of consciousness, level with the heart in the sushumna nadi.

Antar Yoga internal worship in which external formalities become redundant.

anugraha grace.

aparigraha non-covetousness.

apas water.

Arjuna one of the five Pandava brothers, who plays a major role in the *Mahabharata*; the disciple to whom Krishna delivers the teaching that has become known as the *Bhagavad Gita*.

asteya non-stealing.

Atman the Self; the eternal essence of all; the Supreme.

avadhuta a purified one; a spiritual aspirant who commands universal reverence and who has knowledge of the Self.

avairagya absence of dispassion.

avatar (ava-tri "to descend") the direct descent of God on earth; an incarnation of God.

Balarama the brother of Krishna.

Bhagavad Gita the "Song of God"; the poem within the *Mahabharata* that contains Krishna's teaching given on the battlefield to Arjuna.

Bhagavan the divine one; the adorable one; generally this epithet is applied to either Krishna or Shiva as possessors of the qualities that only a god can possess ~ absolute power, courage, fame, wealth, knowledge and renunciation.

Bhagavatham the "Book of God"; one of the Puranas of the Vaishnavite sect; also known as the *Bhagavatha Purana*.

bhakta a devotee who follows the path of bhakti.

bhakti devotion; worship; love; adoration.

Bhakti Yoga the path of yoga that is devoted to worship and adoration.

Brahma the first member of the Hindu trinity, the god responsible for creation.

brahmacharin one who practices brahmacharya.

brahmacharya (Brahman "the transcendent Self," acharya "disciple" or "seeker"); one who seeks to know Brahman; the first stage of life in the varnashrama system.

Brahman ("expansion") the supreme Reality; the Self.

brahmana see brahmin

brahmin a member of the priest caste, the highest order in the varnashrama system.

buddhi (budh "to awaken") awareness; understanding; an evolution of Prakriti.

chakra ("wheel"); a center in the nadis of the "subtle" body.

dharana concentration; the second stage of meditation.

dharma (dhri "to support") that which is established; the law; duty; justice; virtue; the nature or essential quality of anything from a single cell to a human being.

dhyana unbroken concentration, when the mind is completely under control and fixed on the chosen deity.

dvaita ("dual") school of Vedanta founded by Madhva, which emphasizes the duality between Brahman and the individual.

Dvaraka famous and ancient city on the north-west coast of India; Krishna's capital, which was submerged in the ocean when Krishna departed.

Gayatri Vedic mantra; name of a goddess.
ghee unsalted clarified butter, used in Vedic ritual.
Govinda one of the names of Krishna.
grihastha second stage of life in the varnashrama system.
guna the three qualities of creation: sattva, rajas and tamas.
guru one who is unshakeable or unmoveable; one who is established in Self-realization; the spiritual preceptor pivotal to the spiritual path.
Hamsa ("swan") a symbol of the supreme Reality; a symbolic mantra in the form of inhalation (ham) and exhalation (sa) ~ ham is the symbol of Purusha and sa is the symbol of Prakriti: together they are Ishvara.
Hanuman the supreme devotee of Rama, who was the first human incarnation of Vishnu, and of Sita, Rama's wife.
Hari (hri "to steal": "the one who has stolen our hearts") one of the names of Krishna.
Indra ruler of the gods and of heaven.
indriya organ, limb; sense; action; organ of action (like a hand or an eye).
ishta devata the chosen deity ~ the deity used for one's personal worship or as a focus in meditation.
Ishvara that which is; the deity.
ishvara prahidhana aligning oneself with the deity.
jagat universe described in the Puranas; the earth is where karma is worked through and samsara is gained.
Jiva living; anything living; Brahman as the individual.
jnana knowledge which removes the suffering that results from avidya (ignorance). There are two kinds of jnana: bauddha (intellectual) and paurusa (intuitive) ~ it is the latter which is conducive to liberation.
Jnana Yoga the path of yoga that leads to knowledge of the tattvas and the expansion of paurusa (internal or intuitive knowledge).
jnanendriyas the five organs of perception: nose, tongue, eye, skin, ear.

kala time and the doctrine of time; one of the evolutions of Prakriti.
Kali Yuga the fourth and final age of the current cycle of creation.
kalpa age or eon.
karma (kri "to do") action; past actions that lead to a result.
Karma Yoga the Yoga of selfless action.
karmendiyas the five organs of action: reproductive, excretive, feet, hands, ears.
Keshava ("he who has long hair") one of the names of Krishna.
Krishna "the dark one" meaning Krishna or "he who draws us to himself" meaning Vishnu; born in response to a plea from mother earth to be rid of the burden of unrighteousness.
kriya performance of actions.
Kriya Yoga Yoga system that employs purifying rituals and practices.
kshatriya warrior caste in the varnashrama system.
Kurukshetra the battlefield in the *Bhagavad Gita.*
kusha sacred grass used in rituals.
Mahabharata the longest poem in history; one of the epic poems composed in Sanskrit over 3,000 years ago.
Mahat Tattva Cosmic Intelligence.
manas mind.
mandala a geometric shape or pattern that is often "perceived" in meditation and which usually signifies an aspect of the Infinite.
mantra mystical incantation; powerful formula of words or sounds to be recited out loud or internally; the Vedic texts.
maya illusion; false knowledge; that which is limited or measured; that which seeks to limit or measure.
Mimamsa one of the six orthodox systems of Hinduism; more accurately called Purva Mimamsa.
Moksha salvation, spiritual liberation.
nada ("sound") the Supreme Being expressing itself as creation though the first vibration of sound.

nadi meridians of the subtle body through which flows the prana; said to be 72,000 in number; the sushumna, ida and pingala nadis are the most important.

Narayana one of the names of Krishna.

niyama contract with oneself; cultivation of specific personal virtues like purity, contentment, physical self-discipline, scriptural study and aligning oneself with the Infinite.

Om the pranava (single-syllabled) mantra considered to be the most powerful and most sacred of all mantras.

panchatattva earth, water, fire, air and space.

Pingala name of the prostitute in Dialogue 3; one of the three major nadi.

prahvi humility.

Prakriti the principle of creation; the counterpart of Purusha; the origin of the universe.

prana ("to fill") the vitality that fills creation.

pranayama those practices (often, but not always, breathing practices) by which the prana, or vitality, is brought under control.

prithvi earth.

puja worship of a deity or the ishta devata conducted with water, food, flowers and perfumes.

Purana ("ancient") a group of Sanskrit texts, composed in verse, which relate stories and genealogies of gods and sages and have a cosmology of their own; among the most important Puranas are the *Bhagavatha Purana* (from which the *Uddhava Gita* is extracted), the *Vishnu Purana*, the *Shiva Purana* and the *Devibaghavata Purana*.

Purusha the person; the counterpart of matter; the transcendent Self; that which is but is uninvolved in creation.

Purushottama the supreme person, a name of Vishnu.

Purva Mimamsa see **Mimamsa**

rajas second of the three gunas; the force of expansion; creation; passion; energy.

rishi ("one who sees") one of a group of ancient sages to whom the Vedas were revealed.

rudraksha mala string of prayer beads made of 108 dried berries.

rupa the seen form; the outward appearance.

sadhana practices which lead to Self-realization.

samadhi (sam "together," adhi "superior," "above" and "the Absolute") individual merging with the Absolute.

samsara the cycle of birth, death and rebirth.

Sanatana Dharma ("eternal law") the name adopted by Hindu reformers in the nineteenth century.

Sankhya philosophical system propounded by the sage Kapila; the forerunner of Buddhism and the Ashtanga Yoga of Patanjali.

sannyasa final stage of life in the varnashrama system; renunciation.

sannyasin one who practices sannyasa.

santosha contentment.

satsanga association with people of spiritual purity.

sattva first of the three gunas; law; purity.

satya truthfulness.

saucha purity.

shakti power; name of a goddess.

Shiva ("the auspicious one") the third member of the Hindu trinity; the god of destruction; the one who presides over the destruction of the ego (ahamkara).

shudra the fourth caste of the varnashrama system.

Shuka narrator of the *Uddhava Gita*; son of the sage Veda Vyasa.

siddhi perfection; the powers arising from certain of the sadhanas.

sushumna ("the shining one") the major nadi that runs from the muladhara chakra up to the crown of the head; its flow corresponds to the spinal cord.

svadharma one's own dharma.

svadhyaya study of truth.

tamas third of the three gunas; the force of contraction; sleep; lethargy; darkness; ignorance; inertia.

tanmatras the five subtle elements of matter: sound, touch, form, taste, smell.

Tantra ancient religion that predates the Vedas.

tapas ("to make hot") austerities; self-discipline.

tarpana the sprinkling of water in certain rituals.

tattva ("thatness") the parts of creation.

turiya ("the fourth") the fourth state of consciousness that lies beyond waking, dreaming and deep sleep; the ultimate field of knowledge.

tyaga renunciation, especially the formal act of sannyasa.

Uddhava cousin, counselor, friend and servant of Krishna.

Upanishads (upa "near," ni "down," shad "sit") the teaching that the disciple gets when she or he has drawn near to the teacher; the final portion of the Vedas also called Vedanta ("end of the Vedas").

Uttara Mimamsa see Vedanta.

vairagya dispassion.

vaishya third caste in the varnashrama system.

Vamana the fifth incarnation of Vishnu, as a dwarf.

varnaprashta third stage of the varnashrama system.

varnaprashtin one who practises varnaprashta.

varnashrama the law of the Sanatana Dharma, which uses both the caste system and the four stages of life.

Vasudeva member of the Yadu clan and Krishna's father.

vayu air

Veda Vyasa celebrated sage; arranger of the Vedas.

Vedanta the Upanishads; one of the six philosophical systems accepted in orthodox Hinduism; founded on the teachings of the Upanishads; also called Uttara Mimamsa.

Vedas ("knowledge") the sacred scriptures of Hinduism; the direct revelation of knowledge to the ancient rishis; four Vedas remain: the Rig Veda; the Sama Veda; the Yajur Veda and the Atharva Veda.

vidvat-sannyasin sannyasin possessed of knowledge.

vijnana ultimate knowledge.

vimala purity.

vishishtadvaita philosophy of qualified non-dualism, developed by Ramanuja; upholds the Oneness of things but also the reality of all multiplicities.

Vishnu ("the all-pervading one") second member of the Hindu trinity; god of preservation and therefore the one who incarnates on earth as the avatar; mainly worshiped in the forms of Rama, Krishna and Venkateshavara.

Vrindavana the village where Krishna spent his childhood.

yama self-control relating to one's contact with others ~ includes non-violence, non-theft, non-covetousness, truthfulness, non-greediness and sexual continence.

Yama the god presiding over death.

Yoga (yuj "to join") to unite; to make whole; a system of liberation codified by the great sage Patanjali.

Yogi one who practices Yoga.

yuga see kalpa; age or eon; there are four yugas mentioned in the Bhagavatham: Krita, Treta, Dvarapa and Kali. The Kali Yuga began with the departure of Krishna.

❋ Further Reading

Bhattacharya, B., *Saivism and the Phallic World*,
Oxford and IBH Publishing Co., New Delhi, 1975

Bhattacharya, N.N., *History of the Tantric Religion*,
Manohar Publishers and Distributors, New Delhi, 1992

Danielou, A., *The Myths and Gods of India*,
Inner Traditions, Vermont, 1991

Feuerstein, G., and J. Miller, *The Essence of Yoga*,
Inner Traditions, Vermont, 1998

Flood, G., *An Introduction to Hinduism*,
Cambridge University Press, 1996

Krishnananda, Swami, *A Short History of Religious
and Philosophic Thought in India*,
The Divine Life Society, P O Shivanandanagar, U.P. India, 1994

Madhavananda, Swami, *The Uddhava Gita*,
Advaita Ashram, 5 Delhi Entally Road, Calcutta,700014, 1997

O'Flaherty, W.D., *Hindu Myths*,
Penguin, London, 1975

Venkatesananda, Swami, *Christ, Krishna and You*,
The Chiltern Yoga Foundation, California, 1983

Venkatesananda, Swami, *The Book of God*,
Yoga Trust, P O Elgin, Cape Province, South Africa, 1974

❋ Other Seastone Titles

BEFORE HE WAS BUDDHA: THE LIFE OF SIDDHARTHA
Hammalawa Saddhatissa   Introduction by Jack Kornfield, $12.00

Written in a lucid, flowing style, this biographical profile reveals the strength and gentleness of Buddha's character and brings to life the compassion that gave his teachings universal appeal.

BUDDHA IN YOUR BACKPACK: EVERYDAY BUDDHISM FOR TEENS
Franz Metcalf, $12.95

Buddha in Your Backpack is a guide for navigating the teen years like a Buddha. It's ideal for teenagers who want to learn more about Buddhism or for those who simply want a better way to understand what's going on inside themselves and in the world around them.

EINSTEIN AND BUDDHA: THE PARALLEL SAYINGS
Thomas J. McFarlane   Introduction by Wes Nisker, $19.00

Provocative and insightful, this book demonstrates the parallels between Western thought and Eastern religion and what they communicate about the deep common ground of scientific and spiritual truth. Hardback.

JESUS AND BUDDHA: THE PARALLEL SAYINGS
Marcus Borg, Editor   Introduction by Jack Kornfield, $14.00

Traces the life stories and beliefs of Jesus and Buddha, then presents a comprehensive collection of their remarkably similar teachings on facing pages.

MUSIC OF SILENCE
David Steindl-Rast with Sharon Lebell   Introduction by Kathleen Norris, $12.00

A noted Benedictine monk shows us how to incorporate the sacred meaning of monastic life into our everyday world by paying attention to the "seasons of the day" and the enlivening messages to be found in each moment.

THE TAO OF THE JUMP SHOT: AN EASTERN APPROACH TO LIFE AND BASKETBALL

John Fitzsimmons Mahoney   Introduction by Bill Walton, $9.95

The Tao of the Jump Shot takes the reader on a journey through inner and outer mastery of the jump shot. But it is much more than a book about basketball: it describes how to move with grace, prize every action and experience the beauty of life through the simple act of getting a ball through the hoop.

WHAT WOULD BUDDHA DO?: 101 ANSWERS TO LIFE'S DAILY DILEMMAS

Franz Metcalf, $9.95

Much as the "WWJD?" books help Christians live better lives by drawing on the wisdom of Jesus, this "WWBD?" book provides advice on improving your life by following the wisdom of another great teacher—Buddha.

To order these books call 800-377-2542 or 510-601-8301, fax 510-601-8307, e-mail ulysses@ulyssespress.com, or write to Ulysses Press, P.O. Box 3440, Berkeley, CA 94703. All retail orders are shipped free of charge. California residents must include sales tax. Allow two to three weeks for delivery.

❋ Acknowledgments

My gratitude goes to my guru, Swami Venkatesanandaji, who first put me on this path, and to all the other teachers who have kept my feet from slipping. To Swami Narasimhuluji of Sivananda Ashram, Rishikesh, for his help with the beautiful and complex prayers from this text, and his many other kindnesses. To Thomas Cleary for an Introduction that highlights how this ancient spiritual message is still relevant in today's world where materialism seeks to co-opt all our practices ~ including our spiritual practices. To Seastone/Ulysses Press for their care in maintaining the integrity of this work. To Mataji Panna Desai, who with a sweet gentleness also assisted me with the prayers. Very special thanks go to Swami Agnivesh of Arya Samaj and leader of Bandhua Mukti Morcha ~ a tireless worker on behalf of some of the poorest and most voiceless people on the planet. Skilled in filling people with courage, he always encouraged me when my spirits flagged. To Fiona Robertson of Frances Lincoln, whose meticulousness with the work, and whose patience and diplomacy with all of us engaged in it, never wavered. To Uddhava Samman and Kadambari Michaels, for reading the manuscript. To Hermione Evans, physiotherapist, and to Diana and Nick Nixon, massage therapists, whose massage on my torn shoulder muscle made the task of typing easier. To Nandini Daly for sharing with me the teachings of her guru, the great Ram Tirtha.

I thank my friend Uddhava Samman and my daughter Samantha Ife for the loving and generous help they have given me without which I could not have taken the time to write.

As always, I thank brahmacharini Manisha Wilmette Brown for her insightful and careful editing and for putting words at my fingertips when only the images were clear to me. It is above all her loving encouragement and care that make it possible for me to share the teachings of my guru in this particular way.

❄ About the Translator

Swami Ambikananda Saraswati trained for twelve years in Yoga and Vedanta with Swami Venkatesananda, the world-renowned Himalayan monk. He encouraged her to develop her method of interpretive translation of Sanskrit scriptures by seeking their inner spiritual truths. Her published work includes *Principles of Breathwork* (Thorsons, 1999).